Writing on the Wall

Reflections on the North-east

SANJOY HAZARIKA

PENGUIN BOOKS

An imprint of Penguin Random House

PENGUIN BOOKS

USA | Canada | UK | Ireland | Australia
New Zealand | India | South Africa | China | Singapore

Penguin Books is part of the Penguin Random House group of companies
whose addresses can be found at global.penguinrandomhouse.com

Published by Penguin Random House India Pvt. Ltd
4th Floor, Capital Tower 1, MG Road,
Gurugram 122 002, Haryana, India

First published by Penguin Books India 2008

Copyright © Sanjoy Hazarika 2008

Photographs on interleaving pages courtesy the author

10 9 8 7 6 5 4 3 2

ISBN 9780143063148

For sale in the Indian Subcontinent only

Typeset in Sabon by Mantra Virtual Services, New Delhi
Printed at Repro India Limited

www.penguin.co.in

Contents

Preface

This is a collection of reflections and writings—some, edited extensively, reshaped and updated; others, barely touched—which have flowed from my pen and laptop these past years, on issues of personal and professional interest in the North-east, where I travel, live and work. Some parts of some pieces have been previously published in various newspapers and journals, including *Seminar*, the *Hindustan Times*, the *Statesman*, *Dialogue*, *Hard News* and the *Little Magazine* and on various websites. I appreciate UNESCO's gesture for permitting me to use my article, 'A story of South Asia Water Sharing', originally published in UNESCO *Courier* in October 2001.

Much of my writing on the North-east, which still remains misunderstood and unreported (except in the main for what the virtuous would describe as the 'wrong reasons': killings, insurgency, confrontations, underdevelopment, floods and corruption), is drawn from the many journeys I have undertaken, criss-crossing the region since childhood, with my parents and brother, with my larger family and friends, with students, scholars and fellow-journalists, and also as a film maker and researcher, conservationist and analyst, adviser to governments and policy developer.

Much of this travel, especially over the past twenty years, has been on my own, as journalist and documenter, activist and a proponent of alternative policies, although there have been a few memorable journeys in the company of close friends. The worlds I explored, from the Tibetan border to Bangladesh, and Burma to Bhutan, the understanding gained and the lessons drawn over the years, are rooted in these journeys, as are much of the beliefs that have shaped my life in the past decades.

Conversations with the Naga leader Thuingaleng Muivah in a cigarette smoke-filled restaurant in Amsterdam; standing on a tiny, wobbly country boat called a *haat nao* or dug out and watching fishermen at work in the vast sea which the Brahmaputra transforms itself into during the monsoons (and I don't swim); listening to anguished wives and mothers speaking with quiet firmness and restrained anger about loved ones who have disappeared in Manipur; seeing people in distress celebrate the approach of a ship bringing doctors and health services—all these are part of a mosaic of rich experiences which are uniquely individual and deeply personal.

I have tried to share them as much as I can through this limited space, and hope my readers will come away with a better understanding of some of my concerns and convictions, experiences and endeavors. We cannot speak for anyone but ourselves; yet we can try and make a difference to the worlds we inhabit, if not to the greater issues across our earth, through rigorous practice of our convictions and implementing ideas, instead of just talking about them in conference halls in Delhi, Guwahati or Kolkata.

An ounce of practice is worth many times more than tons

of theory: I believe in applied theory, without disparaging those who develop theoretical frameworks. My approach is based on a simple philosophical text: we have one life, and it is for us to make the best use of it, to reach out to those who are less fortunate and apply to reality those ideas which can make the difference that we wish to see.

These pieces convey my concerns on a wide range of issues, from the Brahmaputra and river waters to the peace talks in Nagaland, from the situation in Burma (Myanmar) to the anger and disappointment at the failures of the Government of India, as well as that of local governments and governance. I do not exclude the violence and stubbornness of groups such as the United Liberation Front of Asom.

The North-east, as many have commented in books, essays and voluminous reports, is an extraordinarily rich and diverse region, in natural resources and beauty, in its peoples and their rich social and cultural inheritance, in the resonance of its complex politics and post-border ethnicities. But the place is also extraordinarily tragic in the range of the violence it has suffered and the blood that has been shed in the name of preserving national unity and upholding India's security. Our natural resources, forests, hills and rivers, are being plundered by the greed of the noveau riche elite that has emerged in the region, as well as their companions in arms in other parts of the country, in business and politics, in the underground (read non-State armed groups) and in the bureaucracy.

The challenges before the world of our waters, which I love and travel upon at the nearest opportunity, are special to me. That is why this book looks at them in such detail.

These comprise among the greatest natural resources of India and the world, not just of the region, and are especially important at a time of climate change and global warming.

Some of the political interventions and commitments that are needed in order to create the changes we seek, including making governance and planning, participatory and open are reviewed. One of the essays is on the problem of illegal migration from Bangladesh, an explosive issue that has claimed many lives particularly in Assam, and which regional and national political parties—as well as so-called pundits, in the media and outside—continue to kick around like a political football, ratcheting up the violence of rhetoric and reducing the space for realism, debate and dialogue.

While believing in the need for debate, I believe it is more important to assert the criticality of dialogue to the politics of our region and the world. Dialogue can bridge the divides caused by political, ethnic and other differences. We need to move from the politics of tolerance to the politics of respect for other viewpoints. We need to welcome dissent by embracing it, not suppressing or opposing it as many of our governments and insurgent groups seek to do, not to speak of civil society organizations.

I am grateful to Ravi Singh of Penguin Books India for his encouragement and to Kamini Mahadevan for her perceptive and skilful editing. It is not possible in a book of this nature to focus on all issues; it should be seen as a companion volume, a precursor to a larger book to follow on the greater region. That next book will, hopefully, take off from where the earlier one on the region, *Strangers of the Mist: Tales of War and Peace*, left. Indeed, I am touched by the continuing responses to *Strangers*.

I was able to put together much of these narratives as well as start the work on the larger book thanks to the INSPIRE fellowship at Tufts University in October-November 2006 at the Institute for Global Leadership (IGL), under its energetic and compassionate director, Sherman Teichman, and his wonderful and sensitive team of Heather Barry, Erica Levine and others.

To my many friends and relatives in the North-east, Delhi and other places, who are part of my stories and my life, I owe a huge debt of gratitude: it would be difficult to name all but some must be acknowledged—Sandi Syiem for being such a good listener, Manoj, Vineeta Jalan and Ratan Saikia for their hospitality in Dibrugarh, Preeti Gill for her sensitivity and support; and my teams on the boat clinics for their incredible, hard work which is writing a new chapter of hope for the marginalized of the islands of the Brahmaputra and for surviving my unrelenting pressure and angularities—Sanjay Sharma, Ashok Rao, Amrit Bora, Dulu Buragohain, Hiranya Deka, Abu Kalam Azad, Mehboob Alam Hazarika and the ship crews led by Kapilash as well as the medical staff, led by the tireless doctors—Bidit Gogoi, Bhaben Chandra Bora, Palashjyoti Mishra, Pankaj Choudhury, Safikul Islam, Hafiz H. Rahman, S.M.A. Zakaria, Nur Yeasin, Abdul Warish and Ganesh Chandra Das.

There are, too, our dedicated nurses, pharmacists and lab technicians, Manik Borua and Bhaskar Jyoti Saud for their consistent campaign to save the *xihu*, our beloved river dolphin, my class mate Milan Baruah and his wife Munni for their delightful breakfasts and counsel on the boat clinics, Dr. Jayanta Madhab for his kindness, Dileep Chandan, editor of *Asom Bani*, who always made time, Udayon and Tilottama

Misra, Giti Bou and Baba and Preeti, Sanjib and Tridib Kakoty and their family for conversations, laughter and great food. My brother and sparring partner in arguments, ideas and dialogue, Dr. Suzoy Hazarika, remains a wonderful source of inspiration.

Minal's support has made many things possible over the years; our daughter Meghna's affection and amazing understanding spans the years and across the miles—the last essay, written on 31 December 1990 for the *Hindustan Times*, is inspired by her; Leah, our wonderful Labrador, makes life in Delhi so much more relaxing and happy.

This book is dedicated to my mother, Maya Hazarika, who left us on 26 August 2006. She enjoyed my stories and travels, and, while encouraging my writing and professionalism, kept her own writing and poetry away from us (my brother and I discovered hundreds of poems and songs in different diaries and books at the Shillong home after her passing). Above all, she tried to teach me, perhaps without a great deal of success, the need to be an open-minded and clear-headed human being; it was important to speak out, she felt, but it was also important to listen to others and have both a sense of balance and humility.

Sanjoy Hazarika
New Delhi/Shillong
20 August 2008

INTRODUCTION

Mist swamps the Garo Hills of Meghalaya as farmers plough their fields.

After the Long Night, There is a Dawn[1]

When introducing the Armed Forces Special Powers Bill (1958) in the Lok Sabha, the then Home Minister Shri Govind Ballabh Pant declared that 'certain misguided sections' of the Nagas were involved in 'arson, murder, loot, dacoity etc.' He added, 'So it has become necessary to adopt effective measures for the protection of the people in those areas. In order to enable the armed forces to handle the situation effectively whenever such problem arises hereafter, it has been considered necessary to introduce this bill.'

Some members of Parliament, especially from Manipur, and elsewhere opposed the Act; one of them, L. Achaw Singh of Manipur, described the proposal as 'unnecessary . . . an anti-democratic measure . . . a lawless law.'

The Armed Forces Special Powers Act (AFSPA) in the North-East has continued since. The Committee's essential recommendation, as laid out in both its conclusions and the proposed changes to the Unlawful Activities (Prevention) Act, 1967, (as amended in 2004), is that AFSPA must be repealed forthwith; the gains of the law are extremely moot, its negative impacts have been overwhelming.

Many of the security problems of the region can be tackled by the local police and the commando forces with the assistance of the armed forces, where essential.

But the dependence of the states on the Army must be reduced to the minimum and armed forces should be deployed only as a last resort.

Numerous representations from the public as well as from the Army, Para-military and police have informed the Committee that political problems must be addressed politically and not militarily. These must include the processes of development of participative planning, involving local traditional groups in self-governance, instead of sheltering behind the Army and other forces. As we have noted earlier, there has been a sustained and systematic failure of governance; without the restoration of governance and the faith of the public in the ability of governments to rule justly and provide security to their citizens, the problems may become more acute.

This is a long and difficult task and the pressures are enormous. The Committee does not underestimate the scale of the challenges. But there is no option for the Indian State or the states of the Union. Faltering and even failing, at times, the states of the Union, and especially the North-east, must strengthen their own systems of governance, restoring the confidence of the people and providing the basics of governance.

What started as a political demand and insurgency in the Naga Hills, now Nagaland, has developed into a number of militant armed uprisings in not less than five other states— Manipur, Tripura, Meghalaya, Assam and Arunachal Pradesh. These have international connections with various armed groups and forces inimical to India and democratic forces. In addition, there are the problems of illegal migration into the region, especially Assam. The intensity of the challenges are immense: these range from ethnic standoffs and struggles for land and space as well as political rights.

In the past half century, another major change has affected the violence: on both sides of the 'barrier', the lethality of weapons and their easier availability has transformed the power and quality of the fighting. RDX, AK-56s, machine guns and sniper rifles are used extensively. The immediacy of communications has also effectively changed the profile of these organizations as well of fighting: people can see, hear and even communicate with them by email!

A consequence of such long-drawn out conflicts has been the collapse of governance in a number of the states; the security of the citizens is at extreme risk, from security forces and the militants. During this period, there have been some positive gains—awareness of human rights has increased in India and the world, the media is stronger as are non-government organizations and civil society groups. Violations of human rights by State forces and by non-state armed groups cannot, in these days of instant information, be hidden any longer.

The upsurge in Manipur after the death of Ms. Manorama Devi last June in the custody of the Assam Rifles is a demonstration of this awareness, although there are official views that the agitation was also orchestrated by the underground groups. The latter are not the concern of this Committee, which was appointed last November, as a democratic response by the Central Government to a democratic demand by the people of the state for the repeal of the Act.

After a detailed process of hearings in Manipur, Nagaland, Assam, Meghalaya as well as New Delhi and interactions in

Arunachal Pradesh and extensive internal deliberations, the Committee has reached a conclusion which is detailed in this report.

It is my view that the Army must be deployed in the rarest of rare cases—not as a knee-jerk reaction of governments at the Central and state levels. The army and security forces have, despite obvious shortcomings as are documented and well-known, tried to do their best and upheld their country's honour and integrity.

We have been encouraged by the openness with which people approached the Committee and spoke their views without fear or favour, despite many pressures [they faced]. We also are encouraged by the fact that many of the armed groups in the North-east are in the process of negotiation or seeking conversations which can bring armed confrontations to an end and restore dignity to civil society and the rule of justice and law.

The then United Nations Secretary-General, Kofi Annan said in March 2003 that 'respect for human rights, fundamental freedoms and the rule of law are essential tools in the effort to combat terrorism—not privileges to be sacrificed at a time of tension.'

We hope that the report of the Committee will help in the process of reconciliation and democratization in the North-east, create a space for dialogue and discussion, reducing conflicts and helping the region write a new chapter of peace, change and happiness in its troubled history. We also hope that it strengthens the country's unity, integrity and security and creates an atmosphere for people to live in dignity, honour and peace.

At the end of every dark night, there is a dawn, however delayed. And for every day, there is a dawn, whether we see it or not.

---

[1] This note was written by me on 30 May 2005, as part of the report of the Justice B. P. Jeevan Reddy Committee set up the previous year to review the Armed Forces Special Powers Act of 1958, after the Assam Rifles shot and killed a young Manipuri woman, Manorama Devi, in the Imphal Valley. Her death led to unprecedented protests across Manipur, including the stripping by women in front of the Assam Rifles Centre in Imphal, capital of Manipur. The Prime Minister himself had initiated the proposal and the Committee included retired Supreme Court Justice B.P. Jeevan Reddy, Dr. S.B. Nakade, former Vice-Chancellor of Marathwada University, P.P. Shrivastav, former Additional Secretary, Ministry of Home Affairs, with over forty years experience of life and work in the North-east region, as well as Lt. Gen. V.R. Raghavan, former Director-General of Military Operations in the Indian Army and a director of Delhi Policy Group, besides me. Till date (November 2008), Prime Minister Manmohan Singh's government had neither made the report public nor organized a debate on the Report or even tabled it in Parliament, showing its absolute reluctance if not downright refusal to accept the Committee's sweeping recommendations, which included the repeal of the law as well as dismantling of undemocratic provisions in the other major anti-terrorism legislation passed by Parliament in

2004—the Prevention of Unlawful Activities Act. All who seek peace and development in the region must push for the cancellation of these laws and clauses that put men in uniform above the law and the rest of the people under their heel. Not surprisingly, the Army, the Defence Ministry and Ministry of Home Affairs are the most rigid in terms of even taking a re-look at these unlawful laws. It is one of the worst facets of the democracy we claim, a stain on the image we build for India and an indefensible violation of the equality we proclaim to the world.

One Thousand Years in a Lifetime

Some years ago, I used the phrase 'One thousand years in a lifetime' to express the breakneck speed at which political, economic and social developments have swamped the North-east of India and its people in the past half a century. I am reminded of this during visits, especially to Nagaland, where people speak of the terrific pace of events and feel despair at not being able to control them.

The North-east is a magnificent and tragic tapestry of people, events and nature. You can be touched by its rivers, rain and mist, overwhelmed by the seeming gentleness of its people and stirred by its powerful and evocative history. There is strength and fragility in its immense diversity—there are not less than 220 ethnic groups in the eight states comprising the region with a population of about forty million people. There are communities with kin in neighbouring countries. Four countries abut on the region, which juts out of the mainland of India towards Myanmar, with long borders with China, Bangladesh and Bhutan. Indeed, 96 per cent of its land borders are with these nations. A bare 4 per cent is India's share. Is it surprising, therefore, that people and communities there feel alienated and very distant, not just from Delhi, but the rest of the country?

There are many truths here, conflicting realities, especially in terms of perceptions. Indeed, it is these differing perceptions as much as other issues that lie at the root of most conflicts in the region, between India and its perceived North-east, as well as within the North-east itself.

This is Asia in miniature, where the brown and yellow races meet and mingle, where communities and oral histories span national boundaries as seamlessly as the mountains and the forests which run across them. The only land connection with India is a narrow corridor, the Chicken's Neck, through which natural and finished resources such as oil, gas and tea flow outwards, and consumer goods, food and other essential and non-essential items come into the North-east. There are sensitive and complex problems that have defied solution for as long as independent India has existed.

Our population, about 3 per cent of the national figure, is just above one-fourth of that of Bangladesh. Its peoples are an anthropologist's delight and an administrator's nightmare. A settlement in a district that satisfies one group will alienate a handful of communities in another part of the same district, not to speak of the state! There are special laws, constitutional provisions such as the Sixth Schedule and Article 371A, which seek to protect the traditions, lands and rights of various hill communities. In fact, in some areas, as a result of such protection, no land can be bought by a "non-tribal", even if he or she should live there: there can be no alienation of land.

Sixth Schedule

The Sixth Schedule of the Indian Constitution, when it was launched in the 1950s, was a path-breaking effort to give small tribal communities, disadvantaged by lack of opportunity—educational, political and their population size—extensive powers through the system of autonomous district councils and to protect their traditions as well as their land. To a substantial degree, these laws have worked but there have been other repercussions, including inadequate development, a multiplicity of authorities and, in a number of cases, majoritarian groups in small states, such as Mizoram and Meghalaya, applying pressure on small ethnic groups within their territories, depriving them of the very rights for which they fought against India or a larger state, such as Assam.

Laws such as the Sixth Schedule need substantial change to make them more representative, so that they reflect the interests of gender, non-tribal communities and small tribes. This process should be speeded up. Democracy grows only through continuing democratic practice; what often passes superficially in the North-east as 'traditional' democracy is nothing less than male-dominated fiefdoms and feudalism.

It also needs to be understood that the North-east is not a tribal-majority region. Tribals hold a majority of the land in the hills, but two-thirds of the population lives on one-third of the land, i.e. the plains.

The conflicts between mainland India and its eastern periphery began before Independence and have continued since. People often do not appreciate that one of the reasons that a state like Assam is in India today is due to the courageous stand of Gopinath Bardoloi, the first Chief Minister of Assam, who fought the Muslim League's effort to include Assam and other parts of the North-east Region (NER) in East Pakistan. The Congress Party at the national level would have acquiesced to the Muslim League had it not been for a revolt by Bardoloi, backed by the Assam unit of the Congress Party and supported by Mahatma Gandhi and the Assamese public.

We know so little about each other; no wonder there is so much misunderstanding.

Death of romance, growth of elites

First of all, it should be clarified that today, the conflicts in the North-east, in terms of armed revolts, ethnic struggles or fights against the Indian State, no longer draw on the romanticism and idealism that sustained fighting groups and communities for decades. Dreams have degenerated into nightmares; the fighters have turned on each other and on the people in whose name they claim to speak. The network of cadres, recruits, informers and political leaders is mostly based on extortion and extraction: extortion from business houses and petty traders, from professionals, contractors and politicians. Few are spared. The extraction process even involves government officials, especially in states like Nagaland where officials (who do not pay income tax under special benefits enjoyed by hill tribes) hand over 2 to 5 per cent of their salary to various underground groups. Obviously, corruption would be a problem.

A senior NSCN-IM leader and Convenor of the group's Ceasefire Monitoring Cell, Phunting Shimray talked openly some years back of the organization's taxation policy.

'We collect nominal taxes from individuals as well as business establishments based in Naga-inhabited areas as a contribution towards the Naga cause,' said Shimray, in an interaction with the media at Dimapur, the main commercial centre of Nagaland, in July 2001. He said that the armed wing of the Government of the People's Republic of Nagalim

(GRPN), as the NSCN officially describes its administration, collects Rs 100 per individual per annum as 'ration tax'; the GPRN itself levies 24 per cent of an individual's annual income as royalty tax and Rs 10 as house tax.

Few of the states in the North-east have a stable financial resource base or generate their own revenues; they are almost entirely dependent on the Government of India for their survival from month to month. All the states are identified by the Centre as Special Category States, or states which get 90 per cent of their funds from the Centre as a grant and 10 per cent they have to raise from their own resources (most don't even manage to do the latter); this in turn feeds into a Dependency Syndrome on the Centre, making most states (and all of them, including Assam, are small compared to the larger states of the Union) vulnerable to pressure from and bullying by Delhi.

There are warlords within and without the system. The NSCN (I-M) budget for Nagaland some years back was placed at Rs 44 crore (Rs 440 million), nearly double that for 2000–2001. It has a finely-tuned taxation system which has on record every single business in the states where it is active and it has a tax net for government employees as well. The actual figure for collections is said to be about Rs 105 crore (Rs 1050 million). Taxation or extortion? Depends on who's paying and who's collecting, I suppose. There are those in civil society who justify such taxation, saying that unless peace is resolved and an agreement finalized, 'national workers', the compact armies and the militant 'administrations' need funds to support themselves.

*

The Naga story goes back many years. Let us pick it up on 14 August 1947, the eve of Indian independence, when the Naga National Council declared independence for their people. The fact remains that the Nagas, who did not have a written history or a script until the nineteenth century, when the British colonial power arrived, in many cases preceded or accompanied by missionaries from Britain, America and elsewhere, have always seen themselves as a separate people. It is not my place here to argue whether this perception is right or wrong—it is a conviction which is still deeply held by many people, who also want to live under one administrative roof as Nagas in a Naga homeland that would include parts of the hills of Manipur, Assam and Arunachal Pradesh. This is the oldest independence struggle that the subcontinent has seen, one of the oldest in Asia and as old as free India, although the armed revolt began in the 1950s. The underground fighters have been called many things in the past—hostiles, insurgents, rebels, militants, armed Naga gangs.

The early decades of the conflict were characterized by a certain dignity and honour. Civilian men and women from the rest of India were not targetted; security personnel, camps and convoys were attacked. That ethic hardly exists any longer. It is a matter of shame that during the armed conflict with the Nagas, security forces repeatedly went on the rampage, hurting, molesting, killing and violating basic rights with impunity. In those days, the concept of human rights was not well defined and India's struggle to forge a nation enabled some officials to justify such crackdowns, saying that such actions were necessary to preserve the country's integrity. At the time, villages were burned and rebuilt and many fled their homes to live in fear in the forests. This situation has begun to change for the better and there is a greater sensitivity to local concerns.

The Nagas received training and arms from the Chinese and Pakistanis, who saw the situation as a good chance to weaken India. Other insurgent groups were also supported by the Chinese and Pakistanis at the time: the Mizo National Front (MNF) of Laldenga in the Mizo Hills and the Peoples Liberation Army (PLA) of Biseswar in Manipur. The latter was trained in urban warfare in Tibet. The support from China officially ended in 1976, when Delhi and Beijing resumed full diplomatic relations. In 1986, the MNF signed a peace accord with New Delhi and has never reneged on its word.

The PLA and other insurgent groups in Manipur, such as the United National Liberation Front continue to function and have carved out 'liberated zones' near the Myanmar border, which are occasionally cleared up by security forces in operations lasting weeks, to reintroduce a semblance of civil administration into the region. But there have been at least two such interventions to bring back government in some border pockets in the past years, showing the eroding authority of the Manipur government and even the clout of the Centre.

Chinese weapons are still used, but these are sourced through commercial dealings with gun-runners from different parts of South-east Asia. Plastic explosives are purchased in the open market along with weapons and ammunition and transported by ship to specific points in Bangladesh, and then sent to the North-east or carried overland via Myanmar to Manipur, Mizoram and Nagaland.

Let us move to the present: there are negotiations with

the Government of India between the NSCI (I-M), led by Th. Muivah and Isak Chisi Swu, and a ceasefire between them that has lasted more than a decade. There is peace in the Naga Hills—a fragile peace, but it exists. The tenuous lines of ceasefire ground rules have been framed under a Ceasefire Monitoring Group but not given teeth. Many cadres continue to live outside the designated camps for both groups. The ceasefire is also with the other main faction of the NSCN, the Khaplang faction. But the two factions target each other constantly; there is no ceasefire between them, and there lies the heart of the Naga tragedy.

Yet, this is no mean achievement: that the Government of India, representing a billion people, is talking on equal terms with the most competent of the Naga groups, which has an armed strength of over 6,000 men and women. This is as much a tribute to Indian democracy as it is to the realistic appreciation of both sides that the problem needs a political and not a military solution.

Talks crucial for North-east

Negotiations between the NSCN leaders—who originally flew in from Europe—and the Prime Minister and other leaders become extremely significant in the light of this realization. It is, of course, too optimistic to expect a breakthrough in such a long and intractable problem soon—the talks have gone on since 1997 and continue in fits and starts, with conversations ranging over violations of ceasefire conduct as well as the 31 points submitted by the Nagas, which includes a separate constitution, army and the facility to conduct some level of foreign policy and trade. But the sticking point remains the area of greater territory, an explosive issue which is unacceptable to Manipur, Assam and Arunachal Pradesh—they are not prepared to cede land—and this is an issue over which New Delhi does not wish to risk a regional conflagration. No government, after all, wants to create more problems for itself.

Much is at stake here, not least the future of the NSCN (I-M) leadership itself and the relationship between the Nagas and the rest of India. Sovereignty is out of the question.

The eyes of various insurgent groups, not just of the public and political parties in the North-east and other parts of the country, are focused on the Naga talks. They want to know if a via media can be developed which can meet both the concerns of the Nagas and of India, respecting their respective commitments, dignity and the realities of the situation, especially through a mutually acceptable constitutional arrangement. Yet, any special deal for the Nagas would spark similar demands across the country, from Tamilnadu to Kashmir. But if there is an acceptable compromise, other armed groups could come to the negotiating table for discussions, recognizing the futility of armed struggle which harms their own people and their own causes.

Encouraging in these past years in Nagaland has been the emergence of a group of articulate, committed Nagas from different walks of life who have united under the banner of the Naga Hoho and, at considerable risk and under tremendous pressure, are speaking out openly and in private, in the bluntest of terms, to their 'national' leaders and 'national workers' about public concerns, against extortion and attacks on rivals, calling for unity, reconciliation and better understanding.

This may not sound very significant here, given the context

of Sri Lanka, Afghanistan and Jammu and Kashmir, but speaking out is a dangerous business.

There still is fear of the gun in Nagaland. One cannot wish it away. There is loathing for some of the groups which live by extortion and intimidation. That is why this effort, no matter how difficult and slow, how despairingly tough, of reconciliation among the embittered groups in Nagaland that the Naga Hoho and the churches have initiated, deserves the support of civil libertarians everywhere, of those who support non-government initiatives for peace and democracy. After more than fifty years of conflict and continuing internecine battles, there is recognition of the need for pressure by democratic, concerned civil society groups and individuals on armed groups to resolve their differences. This has not progressed a great deal because many complex histories and much bitterness are involved. But efforts are continuing, including groups such as the Quakers of England and the Baptist Church to mediate and reduce the levels of violence.

The NSCN (I-M) says it is committed to consulting the Naga public and maintaining transparency before a settlement is thrashed out with the Government of India. But this is not an easy task for Mr Muivah. Once, when it issued a statement which, in essence, declared that only it had the mandate to resolve the problem, Naga civil society groups were quick to respond, saying that they stood for consultation, understanding, unity and reconciliation as the bedrock of any future solution.

In Assam, conditions are different—the United Liberation Front of Asom (ULFA), which was founded in 1979, continues to be active but in bursts, with its targets increasingly becoming the vulnerable and poor. Its cadres once located in Bhutan were scattered after a military flush-out operation there by the Royal Bhutan Army in which hundreds of militants were killed, including members of the National Democratic Front of Bodoland and the Kamatapur Liberation Organization, the last being active on the Assam-West Bengal border. A number of important ULFA leaders fell into Indian hands while a handful of others 'disappeared' after being captured by the Bhutanese and then being handed over to Indian authorities. Their families are still looking for them. The military setbacks forced ULFA at one point to start indirect discussions with New Delhi, through a group of selected interlocuters, but this effort collapsed with each side accusing the other of bad faith and lacking sincerity. ULFA has lost support in Assam, although it retains its ability to strike. Its leaders are seen as having compromised on one issue that still resonates in the North-east—the problem of illegal migration from Bangladesh. Key ULFA leaders live in Bangladesh, a country that is not particularly liked in the North-east because of the outflow of migrants from there.

By the middle of 2008, units of ULFA's key strike battalion, located in Upper Assam, announced a ceasefire and called for a dialogue with the Centre to resolve issues. The dramatic move, in the works for months and of which whispers had been appearing in the local media, was facilitated by a former commander of the 28th Battalion who had been in jail and obviously had been persuaded to forsake arms by security agencies. The leader, Mrinal Hazarika, and his colleagues were promptly denounced by a shaken ULFA leadership although the latter also made noises about possible talks.

The impact of the Naga discussions is seen in the Bodo areas of Assam. The Government of India negotiated a deal in the mid-1990s that turned democracy on its head—it gave political power to a minority (the Bodos) and virtually no representation to the majority, non-Bodo tribes and non-tribals such as Bengalis and Assamese. Yet, talks between the one-time militant Bodo Liberation Tigers, New Delhi and Dispur resulted in an accord which absorbed this group into the Indian Constitution and system. This is significant because the Bodos are the largest plains tribal group, known for their opposition to the Assamese, a feeling born out of bitterness at economic and political neglect by successive Assam governments.

The ceasefire with the Bodo Liberation Tigers, which morphed into a political party, the Bodoland Peoples Progressive Party (BPPP), led to an alliance with the Congress and they share power in Assam, with Bodo ministers holding key portfolios such as Agriculture and Panchayati Raj, after the 2007 state legislative elections that reduced Congress' majority but enabled it still to retain the single largest party status—but one which needed a partner in order to form a stable government. The BPPP fitted the bill.

In addition, the Sixth Schedule was amended to enable its extension to the plains area (till then, it had been applicable in some hill areas of the region: Assam, Meghalaya, Mizoram and Tripura) —the Bodoland Territorial Council.

Power may be an aphrodisiac, but it also is a powerful tool to reduce insatiable longings in politics to a reasonable level, moderated by sharing of power and funds. The National Democratic Front of Bodoland, which suffered heavy setbacks in the 2003 military operation by Bhutan against it and other armed groups from Assam based there, is in a ceasefire with the Government of India, although it keeps complaining about demands not being met.

One cannot reflect on the issues before the North-east without referring briefly to that of migration and the growth of fundamentalism. One is not talking here about the mushrooming of *madrasas,* but about the less visible radicalization of young men and women in marginalized regions, untouched by development and what little economic growth is seen elsewhere in Assam. Shut out of the system, they are desperate for jobs and work and embittered by the failure of governance. They live predominantly in Lower Assam although some groups are located in Upper Assam as well. Those in the south and west are angered by the 'Bangladeshi' tag. Generations of them have lived in Assam, studied in local schools, gone to Guwahati University and other centres of learning, and work in government and private organizations. Those who live in the rural areas, especially on the islands and river bank regions, are the poorest, living in conditions of great stress and poverty.

These areas form the soft underbelly of eastern India, especially in Lower Assam where thousands of Bangladeshis move in and out every year, where the breeding grounds of fundamentalism and greater confrontation exist. A response by extremists of the irresponsible right-wing of the other religious persuasion also cannot be ruled out in the Assam Valley.

The sensitive issue of whether Al-Qaeda camps exist in Bangladesh is no longer the point. The question is whether the North-east can remain untouched by radicalism of either kind. It cannot and has not been, especially given the high rates of immigration as well as local growth of the fundamentalist phenomenon.

To meet these challenges, four things are essential: one, the restoration of inclusive governance at its most fundamental and basic level with people, through the existing panchayats and councils, given a participatory role, in designing, developing and implementing programs for their own areas – creating a process of inclusive growth; two, the confidence that indigenous groups will not be reduced to a minority and, if necessary, initiate Constitution amendments and reservations that assure their political pre-eminence in perpetuity; three, bringing antagonistic groups together in the process of peace-building through strong civil society movements as stakeholders, not just governments; four, a series of simple economic interventions through appropriate technologies (solar, veterinary care, micro-credit and micro-finance as well as health and education to close the gap between the socially disadvantaged and those who do have access to health or education) that will lift the 'bottom millions' out of the poverty and wretchedness, the insecurity and hunger, which are their daily companions.

I do not despair, because if we despair we lose faith in ourselves and in our fellow beings.

RIVER JOURNEYS

Villagers relax by a small stall on the river bank at Nagarbera, Assam.

The Bard and the Builder

The Bard, Bhupen Hazarika

In the northern Assam town of Tezpur, a small group gathered in the elegant drawing room of Lakhimi and Robin Goswami, a prominent doctor-couple, sipping drinks and listening to a long-time politician recount one of his favourite anecdotes in the Assam Assembly.

The politician spoke of how a mischief-maker MLA had got another Opposition member, who was quite easy to sway, to challenge the then Leader of the Opposition, Dulal Baruah, in the House on a point of order. An outraged Baruah thundered at his backbencher to shut up, but the instigator was not done yet. 'Press on a point of order,' he hissed at his wavering colleague.

'Point of order!' yelled the member, now defiant, but once again stumped when the Speaker asked him, quite legitimately, 'On what grounds?'

He fumbled, but then his friend whispered again, 'Say, bad grammar.'

'Bad grammar, sir,' suggested the legislator.

The House dissolved in laughter as Dulal Baruah turned purple with rage and gazed balefully at his two tormenters.

The name of the Assembly member is not important, but there is much to be said of the mischief-maker, who was none other than Bhupen Hazarika, who was also the story-teller of that evening.

Bhupen-da, as he is lovingly called by millions, is recognized by many as one of the greatest cultural figures that Assam has produced, spoken of in the same breath as Srimanta Sankaradeva, the Vaishnavite reformer of the fifteenth century, and Rupkonwar Jyotiprasad Agarwalla, the early-twentieth century singer-composer who pioneered the film industry in the state.

Bard and balladeer, poet and politician, journalist, singer, lyricist, musician, film maker, writer — but Bhupen-da is much more than all this. He is a conveyer of romance, passion, universalism and humanism. He has gathered awards aplenty: for his contribution to cinema, music, and culture. Besides, he is deeply admired for reinvigorating the Assamese people, awakening them through his songs, and forcing them to rethink old attitudes. In 1994, he was awarded the Dada Saheb Phalke Award, the highest award in India for his contribution to films.

His popularity suffered a setback when he suddenly joined the Bharatiya Janata Party in 2004 to contest the Lok Sabha elections in Guwahati against two well-known politicians, familiar with the rough and burly of today's politics, a distant cry from the grace of the 1960s. His rivals were Brighu Phukan of the Asom Gana Parishad, and Kirip Chaliha, who had earlier represented Sivasagar in Upper Assam. Bhupen-da lost and took a long time to recover from the blow.

Yet, that cannot take away from his contribution to the cultural and political life of South Asia. He is cherished in

Dhaka as much as in Guwahati. His song on the war of Bangladesh's freedom, *Joi joi naba jata Bangladesh* (Hail the new-born Bangladesh), is a stirring marching tune which was on every Bengali's lips during those harrowing days. His songs are not limited to Assamese and Bengali; and Bhupen-da's rich baritone is equally at ease with Hindi, Urdu and English.

Bhupen-da's internationalism (or 'regionalism') goes further than his vocal chords, as is evident when he talks of his special relationship with Nepalis. He was born in Sadiya and grew up in Tezpur, and says he began wearing the black Nepali cap, which is his signature, when his father died many years ago and someone in the neighbourhood gave him a topi to wear. The khukri pin that adorns the topi is a gift from Bhupen-da's friends and admirers in Nepal.

One of the greatest living cultural communicators of South Asia, he has swayed millions with the power and passion of his voice, and the message of universal brotherhood and humanism, which comes through in his songs. He has a genius for weaving a magical tapestry out of traditional Assamese music and lyrics, breathing new life into the language, synthesizing old and new strands of music, and instilling a sense of pride among the inhabitants of the Brahmaputra Valley.

Bhupen-da showed signs of early musical genius even before he started singing on All India Radio in 1937, at the age of eleven. As a young adult, he swiftly made his mark as singer and composer. Later, he travelled to New York, where he earned a doctorate in Mass Communication from Columbia University. He served in the Assam Assembly in the 1960s as an independent MLA. He has also headed the Assam Sahitya

Sabha, the literary bastion of the Brahmaputra Valley's dominant civilization.

During his time at Columbia University, Bhupen-da was a friend of Paul Robeson, the great black American singer, actor and civil rights activist. Robeson's passionate crusade for social justice and black pride has permeated Bhupen-da's own worldview. Inspired greatly by Robeson's powerful rendition of the song *Ole man river*, he created his own moving ode to the Brahmaputra, *Burha luit tumi*. . .

The waterways of Assam have been a source of inspiration for Bhupen-da's songs and lyrics all these years. 'The Brahmaputra is the lifeline of Assam,' he says. One of his notable collaborations for Doordarshan was *Luit Kinare* (by the banks of the Luit), a mosaic of ordinary tales that was both cheerful and poignant. (The Luit merges with the Dibang in Arunachal to create the mighty sea-like expanse of the Brahmaputra.)

Whereas he had been a legend in eastern India for decades, his compositions for the Hindi film *Rudali* won Bhupen-da recognition across the subcontinent. Perhaps the best example of the humanistic ideals that imbue his works is the song *Manuhe Manuhar Babe* (For man), composed in 1964:

> If man wouldn't think for man
> With a little sympathy
> Tell me who will—comrade?
> If we repeat history
> If we try to buy
> Or sell humanity
> Won't we be wrong—comrade?

If the weak
Tide across the rapids of life
With your help
What do you stand to lose?
If man does not become man
A demon never will.

If a demon turns more human
Whom shall it shame more—comrade?

*

The Builder, Gopinath Bardoloi

In 1999, the Government of India announced that it was awarding the Bharat Ratna to two persons, Mother Teresa and Gopinath Bardoloi. While many in India are familiar with the first name, few have heard of the second.

This is tragic, for Bardoloi was a statesman who, more than any other single figure in India, with the exception of Mahatma Gandhi whose support he won, ensured that Assam remained in India in the critical months leading up to Partition. A lawyer, tennis player, diarist (in prison and out of it), angler and patron of music, Bardoloi's ascendancy in the provincial Congress Party in Assam began in the late 1920s and continued, with a brief intermission, until his death in 1950.

Like other loyal Congressmen, Bardoloi was arrested several times for his participation in campaigns against the British. His early years as a political leader were marked by frequent clashes with Sir Syed Mohammad Saadulla of the Muslim League. Bardoloi succeeded Saadulla when the latter's first regime fell in September 1939. The Congress lasted barely a year in office and resigned as part of the anti-war position of the Congress Working Committee. Bardoloi had formed his first government in the teeth of opposition from Maulana Abul Kalam Azad but with the support of Subhas Chandra Bose and Vallabhbhai Patel.

He was to wait for nearly seven years before he could wrest political power from the pro-British Saadulla. During that period, the Muslim League government pushed through a series of measures that continue to devastate Assam and the North-east. Among them was the 1941 Land Settlement Policy that encouraged land-hungry immigrant peasants from East Bengal to pour into Assam and hold as much as 30 bighas or more for each homestead.

The Congress under Bardoloi fiercely opposed the policy which was to transform the demographic profile of the state. Saadulla was to boast in a letter to Liaquat Ali Khan, at the time Mohammad Ali Jinnah's right hand man, that 'in the four lower districts of Assam Valley, these Bengali immigrant Muslims have quadrupled the Muslim population'.

Bardoloi's greatest test came in 1946: he had just become premier of Assam on an anti-immigrant platform, a position that was reversed by later politicians. The Cabinet Mission had travelled to the subcontinent, mandated to hammer out a compromise formula for Indian independence.

After weeks of discussions, going into stalemate, it announced its plan, advocating that Indian provinces be grouped into three sections. One section clubbed Muslim-majority Bengal with Hindu-dominant Assam. Under the framework of its plan, each section was mandated to draw up the constitution for the provinces in these groups and then assemble them together to draw up the Constitution of India.

This plan would have handed Assam on a platter to the future East Pakistan (because Bengal had more members). Bardoloi and his team, backed by the Mahatma, stood firm and campaigned even against Jawaharlal Nehru and Patel on the issue. Assam confronted and stared down the central Congress leadership as well as the British and the Muslim League. The Mission plan collapsed. Bardoloi administered Assam for four more years before his sudden death. His zeal has not been matched since: Assam's first university at Guwahati as well as its first engineering, medical, agricultural and veterinary colleges were set up during this time. His paternalistic attitude to hill communities drew suspicion from their leaders, although during the drafting of the Constitution, it was a Parliamentary Committee under his leadership that drafted the Sixth Schedule, which provided legal protection to the traditional and political rights of small hill groups. While agreeing that such traditions needed protection, Bardoloi also advocated the opening up of the region to direct political representation.

I often wonder about the irony of it all though: here was the one man who prevented Assam from going to East Pakistan, now Bangladesh, and, with help from the Mahatma and his own team in Assam, defeated the Nehru-Patel alliance that was prepared to let it go. Today, the party of Gandhi, Patel and Nehru has turned its back on Bardoloi's determined refusal to bow to Delhi's pressure to accept the unacceptable– to be dominated by outsiders and illegal immigrants–and has embraced the outsiders as its own vote banks and citizens. The problem has gone far beyond Assam's borders and immigrants today are in large numbers in every major Indian city.*

* See chapter 'Refugees, Exiles and Migrants'.

By the Brahmaputra

By the Brahmaputra, the world looks and feels different. Here the world, in fact, is the Brahmaputra. It brushes aside carefully-laid plans with ease and never ceases to surprise. The discussion rooms in Delhi and Guwahati, the business clout of Mumbai, the noisy parties of the diplomatic circuit, the book launches and intense conversations on human rights and national security, the seeming power of the highest offices of the land all seem to fade away. ULFA, the Naga talks, the problems of Jammu and Kashmir, the National Budget—even friends and family seem distant.

A short distance from Dibrugarh, a town that was flattened by the Great Assam Earthquake (measuring 8.7 on the Richter scale) in 1950 and is one of the world's tea capitals, the river rules: powerful, sometimes silent or gurgling its warnings as invisible stirrers churn the surface, suddenly rising overnight, despite it being winter. It's not supposed to do that—but it has been raining in Arunachal Pradesh, upstream, and the Brahmaputra looks dark, under an overcast sky.

Its mood also seems dark, as it erodes the sandbank where we are located; huge chunks of earth fall into the fast current with a heave and splash. More are destined to fall, their future marked with fissures, as if split by an earthquake. A portent of global warming and climate change, I wonder.

Small canoes go by, with Bihari boatmen paddling—one

had three men on board, although there seemed to be space for only one man to sit comfortably. All were fishermen. The boat came close to the shore and a young man leaped out and ran onto the bank with a rope tied to a short bamboo pole until the rope was tight. And against the current, he started pulling the boat upstream. He, or the others, will pull it for a couple of hours before they rest and put out their fishing rods out for a catch; every day they catch at least five or six kilogrammes of fish which they sell in the Dibrugarh market.

There are the bigger boats too: the large ferries which will trudge for nine hours upstream to take goods, vehicles and people to Oraimghat (a mangled version of Outram Ghat, named after a British general or administrator—which I'm not sure). That's the furthest you can go on the large vessels before the river becomes shallower and steeper in Arunachal. Then there are the smaller ferries that take travellers across shorter distances and bring Bihari and Nepali milkmen and their large aluminum pails and drums of milk downstream. There are also boats which go to collect firewood and the precious logs of sal cast down by the current or by woodcutters up in the hills.

*

The wind blows sand into our eyes and hair. And as we head back to the town by jeep, we find our route flooded with water. The river's fooled us again: it enjoys these sudden victories, showing its muscle and stressing our vulnerability. The Brahmaputra reminds us constantly of the need to treat it with respect, even in winters when water levels are low.

We manage to drive through the new channel: the sandbank has turned into an island and when we return in the evening, the water level is even higher. The driver won't take a chance so we talk to a fisherman, old Yusuf bhai who has been here since he was a boy, and get him to take us across in his dugout. The procedure is repeated time and again, to carry all of those who were on the jeep; in between, Yusuf talks about the Great Earthquake of 1950 and how elephants were swept away in the thunderous waters, along with smaller animals, wild and domesticated, giant trees, huts and people. 'It was,' he said, savouring the moment and look of astonishment on our faces, 'like the end of the world; the sky was filled with the roar of the river and there was water everywhere.'

*

We have built small ships here, the largest about seventy feet long and fourteen feet wide. I feel dwarfed by them but there's also a deep sense of elation at a dream that's taking shape. The hull of the latest boat is ready and is sturdy and shiny, thanks partly to the tar that has been used to waterproof it. The rains have slowed the work but from its shell-like appearance at the ghat at Dholla in Tinsukia district where it took shape, it was pulled downstream by a small engine-driven boat, and now the final touches are being put at Maijan ghat, Dibrugarh —the roof, floors, engine, cabins, bunk beds and chest of drawers, an emergency room to examine patients, lights, fans, kitchen and toilets. It's to carry doctors and health workers to flooded areas with medicines and trained help: during the high water season, roads, village lanes, railways and other land communications are snapped for weeks if not for months.

By the middle of 2008, we were working in five districts of the state with four boat clinics and a fifth in the making. We were already reaching 50,000 island residents on a regular basis with mother and child care, especially immunization programmes and treatment for pregnant women and those who had delivered, and other services. We have planned to reach several times this number by 2009. The idea is to cover people on islands who have never had regular access to health care; the challenge is enormous—there are not less than about 30 lakh of them on over 2,500 islands in Assam, or about 10 per cent of the state's population.

The National Rural Health Mission, the Centre's flagship programme for rural health care, UNICEF as well as the different district administrations are collaborating with us at the Centre for North East Studies and Policy Research in this example of Private Public Partnership. It is also a strong representation of the inclusive governance of which governments speak so glibly.

This is the simplest, the natural solution of taking services to people through the water route—but it hasn't happened in decades, either in flood-prone Assam or in other parts of the country; neither the Government of India nor the Assam government has pressed the suit of inland water transport or what one would more correctly describe as rural water transport. Without the latter, quite frankly, the so-called Look East Policy of the Government of India, to try and connect India's economy and the failing ones of the North-eastern states to the burgeoning economies of South-east Asia and even China, is going to be an abysmal failure. The connectivity by water routes is crucial for the development of the region's economy, especially in the light of this policy.

*

There appears to be a rumble of concern about the possible impact of earthquakes on the rivers of the North-east, especially on Assam. Arunachal Pradesh and Shillong in Meghalaya have been epicentres of massive tremors in the earth's crust, as giant tectonic plates have ground together, causing the earth to buckle and populations to panic and flee. It is important to work coherently and specifically on earthquake proofing and earthquake preparation among rural and urban populations, through an intensive programme of public education, training and workshops involving students, teachers, government officials, the armed forces, local governing bodies, scholars, media and NGOs. Media, especially, needs to be trained in understanding better and reporting accurately such occurrences; otherwise the panic button is pressed only too quickly and too often.

But what Assam and other parts of the North-east must prepare for now is not just earthquakes but floods. Because, if there is one thing that is going to come with absolute certainty in the summer, it is our own tsunami—the floods on the Brahmaputra, Barak, Subansiri, Dibang, Lohit and Imphal rivers, to mention just a few.

In 2004, the Government of Assam and many of its dedicated officers and staff threw themselves into the task of saving and rehabilitating lakhs of stranded people, arranging relief to farmers and others who had suffered crop and property damage, as well as saving towns, cities and villages.

The Air Force, Army, BSF and other paramilitary forces also helped in this enormous task, as they do without fail and without the credit that is their due. They saved many lives.

But man's venality also erupts at such times: some businessmen made huge profits by hoarding commodities and selling old stocks of grains. They have been doing this for decades; calamity is perhaps one of the most profitable periods for the unscrupulous and corrupt.

We need to look, in the dry season, while we still have a grace period of three or four months, at our preparedness to deal with the summer's onslaught. Let's take a reality check:

During the floods of 2005, hundreds of embankments had given way because of poor maintenance or just age—they had outlived their estimated life-spans. How many of them were replaced or strengthened? In the absence of a debate which is critical to the future of flood management in Assam and other parts of India, we need to ask several pressing questions.

One, how effective and necessary are embankments? Where will they work; and where will they fail? What quality of workmanship and what strength of materials (and also which materials in different areas with different soils) are required for them to be able to act as a buffer? In many places the embankment is a multipurpose high ground: it serves as a road during the dry season and a shelter for the marooned in the high-water period. But is it doing the work that it is supposed to do—of protecting people and property from flood damage or is it making the problem worse?

Two, in terms of flood proofing, what has happened to the instructions that a former chief secretary sent to all deputy commissioners, urging them to identify locations where high-rise platforms can be built to shelter people and animals from flood? These platforms should have toilets and facilities for rest and cooking. Has this commendable idea been buried in the dusty files of Dispur? Such platforms, in my view, should be built by local communities in rural areas, using local knowledge of soils and topography to decide what design and materials are best suited to the area.

Researchers working on a project on livelihoods by the Brahmaputra have found a sharp divergence in opinions on who should build such platforms. There is a consensus that such platforms are necessary and need to be done according to local conditions with local skills and technology. But in one area near Dhubri, on the char or island and sand bar areas, villagers are totally opposed to panchayats handling these projects, accusing them of being highly corrupt.

Also, near Guwahati, in a village in Darrang district, people are determined that neither the panchayat nor the state PWD should touch the project, and that self-help groups and villagers should undertake any such construction work. This is not a message about different views on building platforms; it is a declaration of a lack of faith in government and governance, at least in most of the areas surveyed.

Flood management presents the government with the need for better approaches to relief and flood management. There is an ancient Relief Manual, which, in the offices of most deputy commissioners, is in such poor condition that it is falling apart. This holy book needs to be urgently updated and made more relevant, bringing into focus the need for a fleet of good boats which can carry relief material, doctors and medicines. Such a fleet must be the responsibility of governments and the non-government sector, working in partnership, but developed in the dry season.

Then there is the need to ensure that farmers, the overwhelming majority of the North-east's population, have access to two essential things: one, is rice seedlings at transplantation time, because year after year it's these that get ravaged; and two, to ensure that good (and dry) cattle feed is made available and in adequate amounts. I have met many farmers who are traumatized by the death of their cattle, not carried away by swirling waters but killed by the lack of fodder, even grazing areas. This is not just a loss in income, of an investment, of an asset but also a loss in livelihoods and the death of beloved animals.

*

The other day at Guwahati, Professor Dulal Goswami, one of the most eminent scholars on river studies, and especially of the Brahmaputra, was describing how a British administrator had once spoken of the way the river moved easily between two hills in Nogaon (or Nowgong) district, using them as 'goal posts to play football.' Those hills are seven kilometres apart near the little nondescript town of Jokhalabandha, en route to the Kaziranga National Park, Upper Assam's tea and oil country, and Nagaland.

Because of man's intrusion into the floodplains and the river's domain, the Brahmaputra has been steadily eroding the dykes and flood embankments (made of earth, not even rocks or concrete). A few years ago, it smashed its way through the second line of defence (the second embankment) protecting National Highway 37 and Jokhalabandha and was lapping at the edge of the final line of defence, the last embankment, gouging out huge chunks of earth.

It had moved two kilometres inland, its old course visible from the black line on the horizon, an island of silt and sand deposits; the dry paddy fields are split as if an earthquake has rocked the area. The only sight of official assistance or even acknowledgement of the problem is a desultory and pitiful looking row of bamboo stakes, driven into the edge of the eroded land. Steel wires fall away from these pegs to bamboo staves in the river—the bamboo structures were supposed to protect the land: they have been already washed away.

The river dismisses such incompetence with contempt. It seems to know what it is doing—it appears to be searching for the route of the old Kolong River which is gasping for life after being dammed and diverted, barely a few kilometres away, and then travelling down the gradient toward the old town of Nogaon (Nowgong). The Kolong would then become a part of the Brahmaputra. If it goes that way in a future flood surge, then parts of central Assam could be devastated, the highway ripped apart, huge displacements of population could take place and, it is feared that the heavily-populated town of Nogaon, a centre of culture and education, its lanes awash with garbage, and home to one set of grandparents and one side of my family, could go under water.

Neither the state nor the Centre appears to be even faintly aware of this impending disaster. They certainly are doing nothing visible about it, apart from rushing there when the initial event took place. It's a pathetic exercise in non-governance—the public, non-government groups and media need to do much more by way of sustained campaigns to exercise pressure on policymakers to move soon and competently, with appropriate engineering tools, plans and strategy.

*

Outside the office of Saifuddin Soz, the Minister for Water Resources at the Centre, is a map which documents the per capita availability of water resources per year in cubic metres in different water basins of the country. The North-east had 16,859 cu.m; the closest were the west-flowing rivers in the South, with 3,480 cu.m. The Ganges had a bare 1,471 cu. m. Need one say more about the abundance of water resources in the region and lack of it elsewhere and the Government's desperation for damming (and thereby damning) the rivers of the North-east?

Mr Soz met with Arunachal Pradesh Chief Minister Gegong Apang (since ousted) at his office in Delhi's Shram Shakti Bhavan, to hear the latter on his sharp opposition to the proposed North East Water Resources Authority. NERWA is based on a proposal made by Prime Minister Manmohan Singh to embrace all existing river programmes and projects in the region, cover all states and conduct a coordinated approach for a joint plan for power generation, irrigation, and navigation that would bring benefits to all.

Mr Apang spoke for a long time, as is his style, and reiterated his complete opposition to the plan, a view he had dramatically revealed at official discussions in New Delhi on environmental and water resource issues in the region, organized by the Ministry of Development of the North-eastern Region (M/DoNER) and the World Bank. 'He did not budge one inch,' said a senior aide to Mr Soz and the Minister himself, in a conversation with me, indicated that the task before him was not easy. 'From him, I learned that in his view there are problems with Assam but things can be sorted out if Assam talks with him,' Mr Soz said, putting a positive spin on the discussion. He had missed the earlier fireworks, I reminded him, when Mr Apang had stunned the participants at the discussion and snubbed Assam's needs as a lower riparian state which was devastated by floods and high water rushing down from Tibet and Arunachal Pradesh.

Mr Apang had not only thumbed his nose at the Centre on NERWA, he had gone ahead with his own alternative: he had passed a Bill in the state legislature setting up a state water resources authority. The idea is not a bad one, especially the need for states to be consulted and develop their own overall plans for their resources. But it cannot work in isolation. Mr Apang wants to stand splendidly alone and control the North-east water tap from his Himalayan perch. This is not acceptable.

All the states of the region, especially Assam, must mobilize and form their own water resource authorities and then come together as equal partners under the proposed NERWA. With such an approach, the Prime Minister's idea need not go under roiling river waters. It would also give it greater acceptance and a firmer democratic base, with the states taking the lead, instead of having an idea thrust on them from the Centre. This, in turn, would give them a greater stake and ownership in the project. It could also ensure that Mr Apang's effort to divert, if not hijack, the concept does not succeed.

Water Sharing: A South Asia Story

Three of the world's mightiest rivers flow through countries of the Indian subcontinent. Despite strife and war, several landmark agreements have been reached, but fresh disputes are looming in the future.

Regional cooperation appears difficult to come by in South Asia. There have been four conflicts between India and Pakistan since 1947, clashes on the Indo-Bangladesh border and accusations about India's overwhelming influence. When the South Asian Association for Regional Cooperation (SAARC) was established in the 1980s to provide a forum for discussion primarily on trade, contentious topics like water resource negotiations were totally excluded from its brief. Yet, South Asia has a commendable record in the realm of water sharing, developed through a combination of civil society pressure, political sagacity and technical cooperation.

Countries had one precedent in the field. The Indus Waters Treaty, signed between India and Pakistan in 1960, is a landmark as far as water-dispute resolutions go. The dispute can be traced back to the Partition of the Indian subcontinent in 1947. The Indus river begins in the Himalayan mountains of Kashmir on the Indian side, flows through the arid states of Punjab and Sindh, before converging in Pakistan and joining the Arabian Sea south of Karachi. The source rivers of the Indus basin remained in India, leaving Pakistan concerned by the prospect of Indian control over the main supply of water for its farmlands. The newly-formed states could not agree on how to share and manage the cohesive network of irrigation, which was impossible to partition.

Brokered by the World Bank, the Treaty, which covers the largest irrigated area (26 million acres) of any one river system in the world, has survived two wars and provides an ongoing mechanism for consultation and conflict resolution through inspections, exchange of data and visits. The Treaty demonstrates how functional cooperation on both sides is not impossible to achieve, though most other contentious issues remain deadlocked.

New breakthroughs were made in the 1990s over water sharing in the region. In December 1996, recently-elected governments in both India and Bangladesh decided to resolve decades of acrimony over the sharing of the waters from the Ganges, one of the most culturally and economically significant rivers on earth. The breakthrough came after years of political stalemate and bitter rhetoric at the public level, alongside quiet work behind the scenes by water specialists, politicians and scholars on both sides at the non-governmental level. The result was the 30-year India-Bangladesh Water Sharing Treaty, signed in 1996.

Bangladesh, being in the downstream and delta portion of a huge watershed, has been most vulnerable to the water quality and quantity that flows from upstream. The way rivers are used in one country can indeed have far-reaching effects on nations downstream.

When India built the Farakka Barrage in the 1960s, Bangladesh (then East Pakistan until its independence in 1971), helplessly watched it wreak havoc. In the dry season, the Barrage blocked the natural flow of water into the country, causing drastic water shortages. And in the rainy season, sudden water releases caused floods and extensive damage, including the loss of property and human lives.

The principal objective of the 30-year Treaty is to determine the amount of water released by India to Bangladesh at the Farakka Barrage. The water-sharing arrangements, primarily for the dry season, are specified to the last drop and depend on the river's flow. It aims to make 'optimum utilization' of the waters of the region, and relies on the principles of 'equity, fair play and no harm to either party,' with a clause for the sharing arrangements to be reviewed every five years.

Spurred on by the success of this treaty, India resolved yet another riverine dispute, this time with Nepal, in 1997. The Mahakali River treaty settles Nepal's entitlement to water flows and electricity from the Indian side, improving on a 1992 agreement. The treaty, however, has run into opposition from various Nepali groups, who claim it is still unfair to the country's interests.

Although these various agreements point to steady regional cooperation on water sharing, another dispute may be looming on the horizon. This time, it centres on the Brahmaputra, the other great river of this region, which flows through Tibet (China), India and Bangladesh over a distance of nearly 3,000 kilometres. Although no dispute has broken into the open, the issue of information sharing has strained relations between the three countries. The problem is that even the most basic data is not disclosed.

The results have been tragic. In the summer of 2000, a landslide in Tibet caused a dam to collapse, unleashing a 26-metre wall of water that destroyed every bridge on the

Siang, as the Brahmaputra is known in the border state of Arunachal Pradesh. The water then rushed through the state of Assam and, within a week, devastated parts of Bangladesh. Human casualties were light but damage to property was extensive. An effective early-warning flood system is a goal that all three governments must therefore work towards.

According to Indian officials, the Chinese had not shared any information on the build-up of water pressure and the heavy rains in the upstream catchment area of the river, known as the Tsang-po in Tibet.*

Concern is also being voiced about purported Chinese plans to divert the waters of the Tsang-po with the help of nuclear tunnelling. This appears to be a Chinese move to assess international reaction to the possibility of a dam on the river, to tap its huge hydroenergy potential.

Cooperation on river waters could significantly improve the lives of millions of people. In the case of the Brahmaputra, it is not so much a question of sharing the waters as of tapping the waterway profitably for mutual benefit, primarily for transport, commerce and industry.

One example: through cooperation, Assam's famed tea could be shipped downstream to Bangladesh and sent to other parts of the world. Oil from the Numaligarh refinery, also in Assam, can be exported in river barges to meet Bangladesh's energy needs. These simple but effective measures would generate employment and revive the economies of marginalized communities.

---

*   Both sides have since agreed to share meteorological data and set up a committee of experts to review water flows in the river.

The Embattled Dolphin

All of us are familiar with its superb leap out of the water, immortalized in paintings and photographs, on film and digitized media, on banners, glass and stone sculptures and room decorations. Down the ages, the 'sishu' or 'xihu' or simply the fresh water Gangetic Dolphin, which travels the waters of the Brahmaputra and the Ganges in eastern South Asia, has been at the heart of the history, geography, culture and legends of the region—especially of Bengal (both sides of the divide), Assam, Bihar and Uttar Pradesh.

Dolphins are mammals. They breathe air, are warm blooded, give birth to calves and nurse their young ones. Each dolphin is believed to have a unique, stereotypic whistle called a 'signature whistle' and these whistles are thought to help animals that are out of sight of each other to maintain contact.

The Gangetic Dolphin is one of only three fresh-water species of dolphins in the world; for those of us who have seen these dolphins down the years, they remain captivating, graceful creatures beautifying our world. But they remain poor cousins to their better-known oceanic relatives, the sea dolphins that are seen at Disney's Sea World and other entertainment centres, figuring prominently in commercial films as well as documentaries.

The less-known fresh-water dolphin is to the rivers what

humans are to land: the top of the food chain. Scientists will tell you, they ensure a balance in the river ecology—their basic diet is fish and their presence in the river tells us that the water is not just clean but also able to sustain different species in the ecosystem.

But over past few decades, along with other species that man in his infinite vileness and stupidity has harmed, these wonderful creatures are also fighting a battle for survival. At one time, there were five species: the Gangetic and the Indus, the Baiji of the Yangtze Kiang in China, the Buta in the Amazon, the amazing pink dolphin, and the La Plata River Dolphin of South America. Recently, the Indus Dolphin has been classified along with the Gangetic Dolphin, as belonging to the same species.

In 2006, after weeks of surveys, a scientific expedition announced that the Baiji was extinct, a victim of the thousands of noisy ferries on the river, over fishing, pollution and scores of other human interventions—including the enormously ugly Three Gorges Dam that the Chinese love to advertise as an assertion of their scientific and technical prowess.

Today, we must fight to ensure that the dolphins of Assam (there are only about 260 of them left), of the Ganges and other rivers survive. The Irrawady Dolphin, a sea cousin of the Gangetic Dolphin, has most recently been captured in print by the novelist, Amitav Ghosh, in *The Hungry Tide*.

Fresh-water dolphins are strong symbols for the over-exploitation of Asia's major fresh-water ecosystems. They hunt for the same species that human beings seek in terms of food: fish. With his nets and machines, man is a better hunter, reducing the fish available for the other mammal.

So the dolphins now must roam a larger area in the

Brahmaputra in order to feed themselves. The silting of the river means that the water depth is less, especially in the dry season, forcing the creatures to seek out places such as the confluence of streams and rivers which provide them both depth and feed.

Being poor-sighted, the dolphin depends on its sonar system to guide it. While it can make out the older fishing nets, which had larger 'jaalis' (lattices in the netting), the dolphin's system is unable to identify the thin gauze of the monofilament (gill) nets or 'phasi jaal' as they are also called; these become death traps as the dolphins get caught, struggle to breathe in panic and eventually die painfully.

In addition, there are three other direct threats—one is from poachers in Lower and Upper Assam who harpoon this beautiful, gentle creature and use its blubber for fish bait. The light fines and jail terms are not really a deterrent. The other threat comes from the constant disturbance of noisy 'bhot bhottis' (country boats with noisy engines) which scurry across the river, especially at Dhubri, near Bangladesh, driving the creatures further away to seek peace. A third is from pesticide and insecticide runoff from tea plantations as well as uncontrolled urban waste that falls into the streams and rivers.

Over the past years, the Centre for North East Studies and Policy Research (C-NES) has worked with Assam's Forest Department to focus on ways of protecting the dolphin and also involving village communities in their conservation. It is no longer enough just to conserve; if village groups are to be involved, they must gain some benefit out of this activity. Today, we are working with villagers in Upper Assam (near Tinsukia) and Central Assam (near Guwahati) to develop green tourism sites, where visitors are rowed over short distances on village canoes to watch dolphins at play, in the proximity of human activities such as fishing, and in one case, on the Kulsi near Guwahati, sand dredging and extraction, which do not appear to disturb them. The effort is to help develop skills, knowledge and capacity at the village level that will enable visitors to watch the dolphins, sample local food and hospitality as well as handicrafts and handlooms. The vision of eco-tourism in these areas must have the dolphin at the heart of any activities.

Other groups such as Aaranyak are working to conserve the dolphin, with the help of highly competent scientists and researchers. With the strong support of the Forest Department and its Principal Conservator of Forests, M.C. Malakar, we have developed a participative approach for public awareness on these issues as well as for local understanding.

The task of saving the dolphin took us to R.K. Sinha of Patna University who has done exhaustive work on the mammal. We had been disturbed by the reports of kills.

We sent a team to Patna, including fishermen who used dolphin oil as bait. They were shown the alternative—the humble 'petu' or entrails of fish, which are usually thrown away as waste. A process of heating brings out oil that is as effective in snaring fish as dolphin fat and the team has tested this in the Ganges and in the Brahmaputra—with excellent results.

The effort must be now to spread the word. There is a huge economic advantage in fish oil—it virtually costs nothing as you are using waste material, while dolphin oil can cost up to Rs 3,000 for a tin.

We need energetic campaigns on reducing the noise levels

of the engine-driven country boats, with simple technical interventions, as well as for stopping use of gill-nets. More dolphins die trapped by these nets than are poached. So it is critical to address these issues. Over-fishing is making us dependent on chemical-preservative-laced fish from Andhra Pradesh and other states. It is driving one of our greatest resources and attractions—the dolphin—to extinction.

Non-government groups and the government must partner each other to ensure all areas of human-dolphin conflict are eased. The Government of Assam has become an innovator—it has now adopted the dolphin as the State Aquatic Animal, sending a bold clear signal of official commitment. Now it should designate the areas where the dolphins live—for these are outside national parks and sanctuaries—as Dolphin Protected Zones or Areas, with curbs on fishing and human interventions, while allowing non-harmful human activities.

One of the most positive impacts of the C-NES intervention has been the weaning away of the Binns in Dhubri who have been involved in poaching and using dolphin oil. I was touched by the response from the community which now not only has renounced the use of dolphin oil and hunting but also embraced the use of fish gut oil so successfully. Like dolphin oil, the new bait attracts one species of fish, called the neriah, a species of catfish.

Sudama Binn, a stocky fisherman, tells me that the fish oil is drawing two to three times the quantities of fish they used to catch with the old bait. It's cheap, since it is basically fish offal, which has few takers. Plus it's legitimate. The threat of the law for illegal activities no longer hangs over fishermen's heads. As a result, they are earning up to Rs 1,400/- or more per day, representing their best incomes in years, as they seek to rush out of the poverty trap. Today, some of these fishermen are travelling across Assam, popularizing the fish oil concept on their own, sharing their stories and, we hope, bringing about the livelihood and mindset changes that are so critical for the embattled dolphin to survive.

In addition, we would do well to be reminded that dolphin conservation is also profitable: in some parts of the world, companies charge a minimum of $75 per person to enable humans to come into contact with ocean dolphins, look at them, swim with them and even touch them. It is said to be a gentle, enriching spiritual experience. Why can't we do that in Assam?

The dolphin's magnificent leap out of water must remain a source of joy for our children and future generations.

Waters of Hope

Every year without fail, the rivers in the North-east rise in spate and devastate large populated areas in the flood plains, carrying away people and livestock. Not less than two to three million people are displaced or otherwise affected by high water, suffering immense loss of property, crop and livestock, often a major source of livelihood and income. At times, as in the great flood of 2005, two to three times that figure is displaced. We have come across cases where as much as 10–15 per cent of cattle head has perished. Not less than 336 embankments in 2005 collapsed. All twenty-seven districts were hit by the floods, including the hill districts, where landslides and rushing water snapped communications and disrupted life. The flood damage was estimated at some Rs 6,500 crore.

The rivers of North-east India leap and bound down hills. There are not less than thirty-three major rivers, which in turn flow into that greatest of all Indian rivers, the Brahmaputra; there are twenty-two which fall into the river upstream in Tibet and in Bangladesh three more join it, including the Ganga.

One is not reflecting on the power of these rivers, which is immense. Nor how others see that power differently: mention the scale and fall from the Himalayan heights to a civil or electric engineer and his or her eyes will probably light up at the thought of dams and projects that will create a surge of energy. One is not talking about that either.

When we talk about rights, how many of us think of the millions of people in the Assam Valley, and smaller but equally significant groups in the hill and plain areas of other states, who are displaced and hit by high water every year? What of their rights? Who speaks of their indignity except the few stray media reports? Who realizes that in the cacophony about dialogue and development and Look East policies, we seem to have forgotten the persistent and critical challenge before us: how do we enable these poor people to cope with floods?

I am always stunned at the lackadaisical way we approach this problem, showing concern only when urban centres like Guwahati are affected by ingress of high water. I think places like Guwahati deserve to be flooded because its residents, contractors and politicians, as well as bureaucrats, have destroyed the land below their feet—they have emptied out wetlands and built high rises. When the next earthquake hits, don't be surprised by high casualties and no amount of disaster preparedness or fire-fighting exercises will help.

Our basic foundations are eroded and corrupt: how can we build anything on them? So, there are times when I feel that the more floods hit places like Guwahati, the better. It should bring people to their senses of how we are willfully going about destroying the wetlands which act as storm cushions around the region's largest city. And this after celebrating the centenary of the Kaziranga National Park in Assam, one of the region's greatest attractions, when we rightfully take pride in what is touted as one of the world's best conservation stories of rhinos. The rhinos have grown in population from a handful to sixteen hundred (despite the poaching that continues, including the publicized hacking of the horn of a female rhino, which lurched to a bloody and painful death; the images shocked people across the world and led to calls for tougher anti-poaching steps).

Deepor Beel, 40 sq km, an internationally-recognized diversity site for birds of many species, local and international, is one of only two such places in North-east India. It lies on either side of the highway as visitors drive from Guwahati airport to the city and is encroached upon by agencies and vested interests of every sort— a camp of the Central Government's Border Security Force is located here, and a railway line runs through the area; there are nursing homes, private homes and stores, brick kilns. On top of all these human interventions, the beel is swamped by water hyacinth. But Deepor Beel is a storm cushion for Guwahati and also a major migratory centre as well as a nesting and breeding ground for birds. All this is being disrupted. We seem determined to shoot ourselves in the foot by pursuing the path of short-term 'development' that harms us.

What about Dibrugarh upstream? I spend some time there almost every month. It is one of the largest cities of the state and consequently of the region. During the 1950 earthquake, which measured 8.7 on the Richter scale, Dibrugarh was destroyed. Subsequently, an embankment was built with spurs to protect it from floods. At flood time, because of the huge sedimentation load of the Brahmaputra, the river literally laps at the top of the embankment. For part of the year, the river flows at a level higher than the city, which cannot be a great source of comfort for those who are aware of this reality and live in Dibrugarh and its neighbourhood. Nor can they take comfort from the fact that most of the town's garbage is taken to an evil-smelling plot on the banks of the river and dumped, emitting not just a foul odour but also polluting the river and ground water as well as the soil. For years, there has been much talk about relocating the garbage dump for Dibrugarh but the rotting stench near the ghat remains, as do the piles of uncleared refuse, decaying vegetables and plastic bags on every street and street corner. Needless, to say, the roads are a shambles, pot-holed and bumpy, despite the fact that there is a town municipal body whose job appears to be to do precisely nothing. 'Civil society', so vociferous about political issues, government lawlessness and quick to declare bandhs and protests, appears voiceless and feeble when it comes to getting rid of the filth that has swamped the city. City elders are upset but do little. Unless local groups, such as the students, NGOs and others organize themselves, put pressure on the elected officials and administration and take responsibility themselves (e.g., clean-up squads of volunteers in each ward) nothing will change. Such issues cannot be left to government any more—because it can't deliver.

In February 2007, the water was seeping through the garbage, under the embankment and into the paddy fields and homesteads across the area. This is Assam's richest region—tea, oil, gas and, further on, coal. But who talks about this problem and the possible consequences? The previous year, Dibrugarh was saved by hundreds of people from the city, led by young men who had once worked with the militant group, the United Liberation Front of Asom (ULFA), who hurled themselves into a gigantic effort to close potential breaches in the embankments and spurs, working day and night. So far that story is unknown and unheard.

And that is the point: the floods delineate a political process as much as an environmental and economic one. It is the story of the strong and the weak, of the poor and the underprivileged on the one hand and lawmakers and policy-makers on the other, with business in between. In some cases civil society is stepping in to fill the breach. But is anyone talking about dialogue; a dialogue which includes debate and discussion on many issues, not just one or two that come to mind? One can only see enormous gaps of communication and comprehension. A dialogue to be true must involve all principal stakeholders—including the people who are most affected by the strife and consequent problems, not just those who see themselves as such, namely the government and its agencies as well as business.

The North-east is devastated by floods every year. That's a given. In some years the floods are worse than in others. Millions, as we know, are displaced. In 2005, some 336 embankments collapsed. That's also a given. Yet, to this day, there is hardly any public debate in the North-east or in the rest of the country about the efficacy of embankments and the need to find alternatives. Embankments today have become death traps: they trap the water, not mitigate flood. They, as any engineer will tell you, were meant to be palliative measures—short-term steps. Instead, they have become the only way that governments and their contractors think. After all, there is much money to be made from gouging hills for boulders which are used in embankments. Little do we realize that in the Brahmaputra Valley floods are not the principal threat to development; it is erosion that is gnawing away at the lands and resources of people, their homes, and their hopes.

To give a simple statistic: India has some 15,675 km of embankments. Of this, 5,027 km are in Assam alone; that is 32 per cent of the country's total. And the government still talks of more embankments. Clearly, we are determined to replicate failure because there is so much money in it. The Prime Minister's task force which was set up to look into the problem of flooding also talks of the normal engineering solution of more dams and embankments, apart from a national water authority along the lines of the Tennessee Valley Corporation (TVC). But the difference is that the TVC, flawed as it is, identifies the public and environment groups and local governing institutions as among the first and most important stakeholders with which to engage. Talk about water in India and these are the last groups to figure in the government's mind. Water policy and water flows are classified information even though with Geographic Information System (GIS) any decent researcher can get the information he or she wants without going on bended knee to the government. The Prime Minister's task force was not even prepared to look at the issue of watershed management and problems upstream until one of the region's most prominent geographers challenged its members.

So, where is the dialogue? For true dialogue to take place one must have the other prerequisites in place—information and transparency, not rhetoric or 'facts' as paraded by one side or another.

Unless the most marginalized of our people, those who are river-dependent among other groups, are represented at the dialogue table, conditions will not change except through growing pressure and violence. Come floods and overnight people lose homes and farms, livestock and life savings, and are forced to live without the basics of human dignity on embankments and roads for weeks without food security or even a change of clothes. And people talk about freedom? Where is the freedom from indignity for the most vulnerable?

Let that be first addressed by those who claim to speak in our name. Let them participate in efforts to save our people and improve their economic conditions, instead of hectoring us from their safe abodes in foreign countries and abusing those who disagree.

Who speaks for the displaced except politicians and governments in an ad hoc manner? Our policies at central and state levels are knee-jerk and the grassroots organizations working in this area are few and either they do not have the spread or the depth and influence to challenge policy-makers.

Some of us have been pressing for the building of high-rise platforms where people can take shelter at times of flood, with a separate area for livestock. This would restore dignity and basic rights to those who are so vulnerable at flood-time that they share a crowded living space with neighbours and cattle. Surely this is the essence of conversation, understanding and dialogue? If we are not bothered about how people live in conditions which defy the very basic definition of human rights—including safety, the right to clean water, food and shelter—then our policies and projects and programmes cannot work.

We often hear praise about our diversity and inner strengths. Yes, they are there. We (the North-east) are South Asia's third landlocked region after Bhutan and Nepal. Ninety-six per cent of our land borders are with other nations and 4 per cent with the rest of India; the main connection is through the Chicken's Neck or the Siliguri Corridor. This sliver of land is our economic lifeline—gas, oil tea and other goods flow in pipelines and over roads and railways; commodities flow into the region through here.

Yet, when the floods erupt in North Bengal and the North-eastern region, road and rail links get snapped with unfailing regularity. These cause huge disturbances in the local economy because it is not just Assam which depends on these imports and exports: it affects all the states of the region where the rail and road routes go through Assam, from Moreh on the Manipur-Myanmar border, to Gelling on the Tibet-Arunachal frontier, to Parwa in Mizoram touching Myanmar and Agartala in Tripura on the Bangladesh border. Our manufacturing bandwidth, if we can call it that, is small: the enclave industries of bamboo and timber, oil, gas and tea.

These days that profile has expanded slightly, to cosmetic products and pan masalas and mosquito repellents. Our strengths of handicraft and handloom are still not high value, although it is proposed that with the National Bamboo Mission some 20 million tons of bamboo can be harvested every year and lakhs can be employed in this field. But there seems to be a lack of urgency at the ground level: the gregarious flowering of bamboo has begun although the administration appears better prepared than in the past and there are no reports of food scarcity. Also there is just a two-year period when it can be harvested.

As we think and look out of the box, we must recognize that the region still imports almost everything—from razor blades and fish to pencils and food grain, from cars to television sets. We are essentially a market and not a production centre. Our fruits, vegetables and even cattle are exported to Bangladesh and Myanmar but there isn't a single major processing unit to tap this existing opportunity. There is little or no value addition. We're just a highway for commerce, not a manufacturing region that goes beyond the basics of transit. We ship processed goods from other parts of India to our neighbours; only raw materials and goods go from our area—such as coal and limestone, fruits and vegetables. Investors from South-east Asia and other parts of the world will not rush to help us; there is little or no altruism in business. Without participative growth and local business partnerships with outside groups (domestic and foreign), we will not go far.

The Government of India's Look East policy is extremely commendable and worthy of support. However, the policy and a lot of the thinking around it—connecting the region to South-east Asia and our neighbours—overlooks one basic point. Without a water transport policy that provides for capability to move large volumes of goods by river, the Look East policy will run into the sandbanks of the Brahmaputra. How can any policy work which does not even consider the most basic of problems: when the region and its main road and rail corridor are under water or affected by water (either hit by it or recovering from it) for anything between five to eight months of the year?

Railways and roads have their spokespersons and lobbies, but who speaks for inland water transport, the most neglected of our transportation systems? Yet, just look at the map of the region—can we not attribute the collapse of our economies and our fall from the fourth place in the order of India's states' income to fourth from the bottom, in the company of Bihar and Orissa, to our comprehensive failure to fashion a people-participative response to floods and high water? And high dams are not the answer— certainly not in a highly geologically unstable and seismic zone like the North-eastern Region. Our experience of the Manas River demonstrates what can happen even in a non-earthquake situation, when a landslip blocked a tributary of the river in Bhutan and before Indian and Bhutanese engineers could decide what to do about it, the earthen wall gave way and a surge of water rushed toward a dam site in Assam. Panicky engineers released the water, giving people little time to evacuate and reach high ground. For after some time, there was no high ground.

Similar events are reported with increasing familiarity on rivers flowing down from Arunachal Pradesh, raising major questions about the harm and lack of sustainability of large dams and their accompanying structures, despite the lung power of their powerful advocates, in the media, among engineers and scientists and among scholars.

The Central Government, in association with the World Bank, is coming forward with a plan to build over 160 large dams in the region. Where is the dialogue here? Were the people of the region consulted? And if there is no process of consultation, then one can foresee a series of conflicts erupting over rights, threatened identities and spaces. One hundred and sixty dams and an equal number of conflicts—is the Government of India and the region prepared for such a disaster in addition to the existing confrontations?

Massive interventions are being planned, proposed and implemented across the rivers of the North-east. But the impacts on human habitation, on existing eco-systems which hold the delicate balance between the health of a society and catastrophe, on aquatic life, on the endemic fish species of the region, on the fresh-water river dolphins, one of the most endangered fresh-water mammals in South Asia, of which there are less than 300 in Assam, have not been studied.

The reasons for hope lie in addressing issues head on, in thinking innovatively and out of the box but with our feet on the ground and with commitment, as well as by bringing in people-centric policies which can be implemented simply and with the involvement of those they seek to benefit.

GOVERNANCE AND PARTICIPATION

Hope—the health team on Akha, the innovative health clinic in Dibrugarh district, Assam, leaves for a series of camps, taking health services where none have existed.

Innovation, Realism, Participation

In 2005, during the toughest season of the year—the monsoons—a team of 100 enumerators in eight states of the North-East conducted a visioning exercise, focusing on the rural population, on what people wanted to see in their lives fifteen years later. This survey covered virtually every district, and over 40,000 rural households. As team leader, I realized that this was the first time that anyone had come to these rural citizens, to seek their opinion on anything, especially on planning for their future. They were asked about their dreams and where they wanted to see a difference: health, education, governance, communications, agriculture development and rural development.

The survey clarified one thing—that minimum needs were yet to be met, despite all the funds that had been poured into the region (a staggering estimated Rs 1,20,000 crore in both Plan and non-Plan projects between 1992–2005). For most households, health and education were top priorities. In addition, there were concerns about new livelihood opportunities and food security. Governance was seen as critical and received lowest marks in the survey, but the interest in being involved in planning, reviewing and implementing government projects that had an impact on their lives was encouraging. Sixty years after Independence, barring some parts of India, most regions, especially places like the North-east which have been chronically unstable and devastated by both natural and man-made disasters, remain cut-off from the basics of good governance and transparency. Through the exercise we conducted, public participation was asserted as critical and at the heart of responsive governments and policies.

The region is among the most complex in Asia, with over 200 ethnic groups and as many languages and dialects. Just this one characteristic makes governance under the standard administrative format developed from colonial times, extremely difficult because different local conditions demand different responses. Then there is the problem of insurgencies and militancy, seeking separation from India or greater rights or just recognition. There is migration, largely from Bangladesh, and cross-State movements from Bihar. Large populations are on the move, creating new fault-lines in traditional societies.

To complicate matters here are not less than eight States with a population of 40 million or less than 3 per cent of India's population; barely 4 per cent of the region's land borders are with India. Myanmar, China and Bangladesh and even little Bhutan have longer borders with the North-east than mainland India. In such a complex region, with burgeoning demands from a wide range of groups, a look at the issues of public participation and involvement in governance and service delivery is important. This is not made any easier by the different constitutional structures in place.

Recognizing the unique characteristics of the North-east, law makers have created a web of interventions: thus, while Arunachal Pradesh, the plains of Assam, Tripura and Manipur are covered by the 73rd and 74th Amendments, with Panchayati Raj in the rural areas and municipal committees in the urban centres, there are special constitutional provisions for Nagaland, Meghalaya, Mizoram and the hills areas of Tripura and Assam which seek to give greater powers to local institutions. The Panchayati Raj (PR) system does not apply to these specific areas. What works, to make matters more challenging, are not just constitutional arrangements which came into effect with the adoption of the Republican Constitution in 1950 but also traditional institutions which are respected by local communities and go beyond the space created for constitutional authorities.

In Meghalaya, the State government depends on the village durbars or councils of village elders among the Khasis when issues at the rural level have to be discussed, decisions taken and implemented. The Khasis have a finely structured system of advisers; there are other institutions, for example, in Nagaland with tribal associations, clubs and organizations. There are arrangements in place such as Article 371A of the Constitution under which Nagaland is not covered by legislation passed by Parliament unless enacted by the State legislature, not dissimilar to Article 370 and the status of Jammu and Kashmir.

Yet, even right-wing parties like the Bharatiya Janata Party while constantly demanding the revocation of the 'special' status of Kashmir make little or no mention of that of Nagaland. Either the BJP is unaware of the situation, which is most unlikely since it has shared power with regional parties in the state, or it is prepared to compromise in this case and use the existing political unrest to grab a stake in local power play. In addition, there is another major statute which governs people in the region: the Sixth Schedule for Meghalaya and Mizoram as well as two hill districts and the Bodo Territorial Council in Western Assam and the Tripura Tribal Autonomous District Council area in Tripura.

Under the Sixth Schedule, tribal communities are technically protected from land alienation (by plains dwellers) and can set up Autonomous District Councils which function as the second tier of governance, with control over several subjects. They rarely do much apart from being a training ground for ambitious politicians wanting to graduate to the State level and beyond. At the village level, there are disturbing accounts of tribal elites buying out poor marginalized farmers in Meghalaya and acquiring their lands. States and policy-makers have gone wrong in the North-east by not giving traditional institutions a constitutional role in governance, especially at the rural level. This would have enabled them to access funds and implement policies but also make them accountable to the public, instead of operating as gender-insensitive fiefdoms.

Decades have passed and it is only now that a discussion, if not a full debate, is taking place on delivery and governance mechanisms in the region. Views are growing louder that seek the involvement of traditional institutions, but with extensive reforms, including accountability, gender representation and democratic change—not selection by a clan or nomination by male elders.

In some tribes, for example, the male chief owns all property and can do with the land as he wishes. And even though societies such as the Khasis and the Garos of Meghalaya are matrilineal (inheritance rights go to the daughter), women have little voice in political decision-making: they are not part of the councils although civil society groups are now demanding that right, pointing to the advantage their contemporaries have under panchayats elsewhere. Such views have been strongly resisted by many traditional institutions, although this too is slowly changing. Two pioneering institutions and innovations were launched by two IAS officials: one, in the 1980s, kicked off the village development boards in Nagaland.

A.M. Gokhale, former Secretary, Ministry of Mines, and former state Chief Secretary, saw the need to devolve development funds to village levels instead of keeping these at State and district capitals. This has worked to an extent, but the second step for decentralization which gave it a strong push forward, came in the form of Raghav Pandey's Communisation Programme.

Raghav Sharan Pandey was then Chief Secretary of the State and later moved to Delhi as Secretary in the Ministry of Steel. In 2008, Pandey was honoured by the United Nations for his innovative work in developing participatory governance in an extremely challenging environment. Pandey looked at the biggest asset of the Nagas, their social capital, and proposed a structured approach that would give villagers control over State assets—thus, for example, teachers would be paid through a bank account in the village, not the State treasury; the local government school could take independent decisions on construction.

The programme is now mandated by law—it may not be working as well as envisaged but provides a flexible, innovative way of developing participatory governance. It has now been extended to the power sector. These are lessons which could be absorbed, not just by other parts of the North-east but the country. With better governance, involving reformed traditional institutions and enabling local decision-making, many of the conflicts and bitterness could be reduced, if not ended, assuaged, if not resolved.

Partly because of this failure, we have paid heavily in terms of lives and time lost, energy drained, economic devastation and social disintegration. Another way is to ensure a tough review mechanism of government projects, both state-wise and national, that are scanned for quality, integrity and levels of implementation by groups set up by government especially for this purpose. While the Right to Information can have a role in asserting transparency and meeting public demands for accountability—even though in numerous cases, officials have done their best to block review through subterfuge and even intimidation—governments need to have a structured form of review and independent assessment.

This could take the form of a Review Committee that includes a representative of the principal stakeholder, the state or Central Government or public sector undertaking or even funding agency such as the North Eastern Council, a technical specialist (since many of these projects are infrastructure-related, this is an important element; the specialist should be drawn from outside the state where the review is planned); a financial specialist to look at the financial procedures and accounting practices; a representative of a prominent NGO and a respected local leader.

Such a structure should be built into every project valued at above Rs 5 crore (50 million rupees) that is State-funded and would increase the involvement of local communities not just in project planning and conceptualization but also in their implementation and sustained running. The findings of the review would be released to the media, put on the organization's website and otherwise disseminated. It would be a learning experience all around and strengthen democracy and governance.

Another example comes from the North Eastern Region Community Resource Management Project (NERCORMP), which started in six districts of Assam, Manipur and Meghalaya, was sponsored by the North Eastern Council and involved the International Fund for Agricultural Development (IFAD). That project is now to cover over fifty districts in the entire North-east, based on its record of good delivery and governance mechanisms through participatory programming. Examples from this project have shown that unlike government schemes, these have not been afflicted by the malaise of extortion primarily because they are community-driven and people-owned. This vindicates the notion that many systems can co-exist if delivery mechanisms work.

Toki Blah, a former IAS officer from Meghalaya and a consultant from Shillong, says that the IFAD program and the village development institutions established under the project, Natural Resource Management Groups (NaRM-Gs) (which are elected both from traditional institutions and the general population, including governmental institutions and employees—usually traditional institutions and government are at daggers drawn) 'offer a viable example of empowered communities who undertake overall development work at the grassroots level. Drinking water for the community is also taken up under resource management of the NaRM-G'. Activities for ensuring sustainable water supply involve a one-time contribution per household for maintenance cost and the banning of jhumming (slash and burn cultivation) in water source catchment areas. At every NaRM-G meeting (once a month), a maintenance cost of Rs 5–10 is contributed by every group member. In addition, and this is critical across the region, the program is gender sensitive—two persons from every household, a man and a woman, make up the general membership. These are examples worth emulating.

Complex problems do not necessarily require equally complex answers; sometimes, simple steps pave the way for change and resolution. This is where a decentralized approach to the ethnic weaves and demands of the North-east has been missing. The suggestions made here can play a role in the inclusive development, greater democratization and calming of the region.

The Writing on the Wall

The North-east sits on a rapidly exploding urban disaster. Its cities are among the fastest growing in the country but, like other Indian cities, civic measures such as sanitation and water supply, not to speak of electricity, have fallen far behind the rush to build.

The official residences of two deputy commissioners in the district of Kamrup, for example, are located right on the banks of the surging Brahmaputra, housed in beautiful old British-built bungalows with high ceilings, teak floors and beams and jaali netting verandahs to keep out the persistent mosquitoes. Guwahati, the region's largest city, is in Kamrup, the state's most populous district. Many residents have come and gone through these bungalows over the past century. They have beautiful views of the river, of sunrises and sunsets. They also are witness to unending urban pollution, destroying the health of the river as it flows along the city, with untreated muck of every kind tossed into it.

One of the great water resources of the world, the Brahmaputra is celebrated in music and ballads but treated as a garbage dump by city dwellers. There are 'parks' for walking along one particular stretch of the river front between the old Cachari vegetable bazaar, where fresh vegetables and fruits come by the boatload from across the river, and the

Kamrup (Rural) Deputy Commissioner's bungalow, which are particularly worth noting as they are a telling commentary on the impotence of the government and the total failure of citizens to save their city and their river.

One park is in a somewhat decent condition: it has walkers, yoga practitioners and even a new prayer and discussion group, which I have just seen. I have walked here for over twenty years. It has tree cover, a walking trail, a few benches, one short, dilapidated wooden jetty, observation points, and two cement jetties, which take a visitor above the riverbank. The park is maintained by the Assam Tourism Development Corporation. A couple of old rusted boats sit silently below. Pieces of plastic are strewn around and the sight of people on the banks some distance away, urinating and even defecating is offensive. Entry costs Rs 2/-. But there isn't anyone to whom I can make a payment.

Whenever in Guwahati, I walk down the hill at the Bellevue hotel, past the largely Bihari (they're still around, they haven't left, despite ULFA's threats and killings) and Bengali settlements—a little row of shops, shacks and mandirs—and slow down at the Ujan bazaar fish market— here fresh fish, often still flopping, lie in baskets, tin drums and plastic thelas—and savour the sights as boats come in with a new catch. The bustling fish market, one of the oldest in the city (it is said to be over 150 years old), sees peak business in the early hours of the morning.

A short distance from the fish market is another park, which was funded, a notice grandly tells you, by a former Rajya Sabha member. First there's an area where straw is stored and sold. The boundary walls are broken. There are a bunch of cycle rickshaws parked here; a row of huts of tin and thatch look out upon the river. Children play, quarrel and run about; men and women keep moving in and out.[3]

Contrast that with the beautifully-painted old Assam-type bungalow, a wooden building with blue paint, and the new apartment blocks plastered with cement and freshly-painted doors and windows, a reflection of the new rich, as one moves towards the planetarium. The Brahmaputra is a constant companion, gentle in winters, with huge shoals and sandbanks or saporis and chars, newly-emerged and old. If ever there was a case of trespass and damage to the environment, to a public place, this is it.

The Kamrup (Rural) DC's official bungalow is a short walk from here, past a couple of open sewage points which pour the poison of the city's untreated garbage into the river. It is a moot point whether the bungalow's resident is either aware or concerned about the violation of law and the disaster in front of his or her very eyes. This is not an issue of the position held, but whether the concerned officer also considers himself or herself as a citizen with rights and duties.

If officers, with such wide-ranging powers do not act, what can the citizen expect in terms of services, barring filth and bad governance at every level—the city's drains are clogged and overflowing with rich red soil washed down from the hills, hit by fresh land cutting to accommodate new, illegal construction. Incidents like these are multiplied across Guwahati and other burgeoning urban centres in the North-

---

[3]   The huts were demolished in a clean up campaign in the summer of 2008 but I am sure that either they will be back, eventually, or their inhabitants have been settled, for the moment, in another part of the city.

east.The sewer lines flow down the bank from under the park (there is a third further down on the road). The discharge is not piped; it is not even treated. The filth of the neighbourhoods bordering the river flows down the banks in a black, vicious, bilious slush that spews into the gentle green-brown water. For hundreds of metres down the bank, the line of filth wounds the river, but then the Brahmaputra, in its infinite grace, power and majesty, absorbs the injury and heals it. A few hundred metres down, the river appears restored to its original state.

Across the city and along the cities and towns which lie by the Brahmaputra and its tributaries, this scene is repeated scores of times. Yet, how much can nature heal the wounds persistently inflicted by the venality of humans? Who is looking at this? Are environmental scientists, government environment officials and their research teams trudging to these sites, collecting water, analysing samples and making not just recommendations but also ensuring that treatment plants are installed and used. There is no point of just talking about these issues any longer—the reality is visible, the warnings are clear, the writing is on the wall. One would expect that the local municipal councillors in Guwahati and other towns across from Assam, irrespective of party affiliations, will follow up on this. Election results from all states stress one basic lesson for candidates: deal with local problems, provide some governance, otherwise you're out.

*

Another classic case is Shillong, once the prince of hill stations, which boasted of horse racing, and a fine golf course (called the Gleneagles of the East) and where the wind sang through its pine forests. Today, ugly concrete structures soar where pines once stood, displaying the relentless accumulation of wealth by government officials (some retired and some still in service) and politicians. Despite these grand monstrosities, some beautiful old family-owned buildings still survive, although the trend is to destroy classic homes of wood and replace them with ones which personify cemented ugliness.

There is no effort by NGOs or civil society here or anywhere else in the North-east to preserve heritage buildings, which are overwhelmed either by decay or disuse or worse still, destroyed by insensitivity and the hunger to rebuild and display wealth.If the media and civil society groups do not even focus on these issues, which concern our past and the way we wish to build our future, then they are failing in their basic responsibilities.

The student organizations of our region, instead of calling bandhs and protests on every political issue worth flogging, should look at some of these real concerns, which affect people today and will impact generations to come.The streets are clogged with heavy traffic at virtually all times because there is no regulation on the issue of permits and licenses. And school opening and closing times in Guwahati and Shillong are nightmares. The traffic and tree felling has ensured that hill towns have become much warmer over the years and damaged water sources, hill streams and natural aquifers. There is hardly any sewage control worth the name in Shillong and much of the untreated raw effluents pour into the scenic Umiam Lake, fourteen kilometres downhill, better known as Barapani, a water body created by the construction of a hydro-electric dam in the 1960s.

Many of the holidayers, picnickers and punters don't know it but the lake is highly contaminated with Shillong's muck. The water levels at Umiam are low in spring and early summer; as a result electricity generation has dropped and the energy-surplus city of Shillong now suffers from power cuts, though after midnight! Worse affected are smaller district towns, slowing work in the offices of government and other levels. It is important to de-silt the lake in order to revive it, clean it and create greater storage space for fresh water.

A Shillong bypass—both literally and metaphorically—has been stalled for many years and no major political leader from the state or the region or any member of parliament or organized CSO (civil society organization) has been effective in ensuring the project's implementation, although this is, in sheer economic terms, the most significant route of the entire North-east, with more vehicles plying on it with goods and passengers, groaning and whining up steep hills, than on any other highway. The trucks are invariably overloaded and, not surprisingly, often break down, thereby creating traffic jams and hazards en route the winding route—and many frustrated travellers.

Urban centres in the North-east need many things. Let's start with just three—the first is a strong civic awareness starting from the school level that seeks to reduce and stop the indiscriminate dumping of waste—this is where individuals and organizations are critical; second, they need waste disposal sites and systems, which is the role of government; and third, they require a partnership between the public and private domains so that sustainable processes remain in place and towns and cities such as Guwahati and

Shillong become a source of pride and joy, not of despair and frustration.

*

Another unseen but growing gangrenous wound in our urban centres is the rise in domestic violence, despite proclamations of gender equality in the region, and the dark and vicious trend of child abuse.

The other day, my friend Sandi Syiem told me a story of Shillong which filled me with sadness, anger and horror. A young mother had come to see him, Sandi said, with her two children, a boy of six and a girl who was five. 'I was asked to see you because I was told you could help me,' she said. It turned out that both children had been sexually abused, not at home, but by a molester who was roaming free in the neighbourhood. It also was clear soon enough that other children, too, had been victims of this abuser.

It is not a picture I have imagined of Shillong, a town where I grew up and which I know well and where some of my closest friends live. Sandi is one of them; he is a psychiatrist and counsellor and has set up, what I think is one of the finest rehabilitation centres in the country for the mentally challenged and substance abusers. San Ker, located peacefully amidst the pine trees and gentle meadows on the edge of Shillong's Golf Links, is en route to the North Eastern Hill University.

Sandi called a lawyer in Guwahati and was told that the man could be put behind bars under specific sections of the Indian law which are tough on such brutality. The woman had not lodged any complaint, but my friend was appalled when she told him that when she had approached the traditional headman of the neighbourhood, the latter encouraged her to compromise. In addition, he told her, other families of victims had 'compromised' and had signed a note saying that they had no complaints. The headman, too, appeared complicit. She refused to cow down and, having heard about Sandi, turned to him. He called Child Line, a centre dedicated to assisting children who have faced physical and mental abuse.

To my surprise, there was a centre in Shillong, showing the spread of the problem. It was also an indicator of how extensive child abuse could be in the entire region, where children are especially vulnerable at times of conflict. Despite the best efforts of Child Line, Sandi and others, the abuser got away with a mild rebuke, partly because of the stigma attached to victims of such abuse. The man may need counselling and psychiatric help but, for a start, such people need to be off the streets so that children need not fear their innocence and are able to enjoy their right to play, laughter and joy.

Yet, Sandi says, there are many more such men, young and older, who are moving about unchallenged, intimidating and sexually abusing the weak and frightened. The problem of child abuse needs a strong close look by health specialists and also by the media in the region, which often focuses on irrelevant issues. It requires extensive research and investigation as well as documentation so that people are made aware of the viciousness that surrounds them and their children, that they are forewarned and prepared to deal with the issue. People need to know who to approach for help and also how they can tackle child abusers and those who shelter them.

It is a major challenge, and not as well-funded or publicity-oriented as HIV/AIDS, but it is a brutal side of life which destroys the very meaning of childhood and cannot be wished away by those who merely extol the beauties of its region, and wish to promote its 'rich heritage' and the fine qualities of its people while refusing to acknowledge the ugliness within.

CONFLICT CHRONICLES

In the aftermath of a riot between rival ethnic groups in Goalpara district, Assam, a police officer tries to calm a crowd.

Waking and Walking Nightmares

Pradip Phanjoubam, one of the North-east's most passionate and sensitive journalists, once wrote of the fear in which people live, of the waking and walking nightmare that life in parts of Manipur has become. He spoke of the kidnapping and death of a young trader by an underground organization, of brutal torture by the police of a former 'u.g.', as the underground or insurgent cadres are called by government authorities and of Manipuri society's rapid descent into a tragic and embittered hell of its own.

This unfortunate, beautiful and tragic state is split by ethnic disputes, territorial concerns, human rights violations, violent insurgencies and powerful state agencies. Fear and deep suspicions characterize life here and these are not quantifiable things which can be measured and 'fixed'. They need sensitive handling, firm leadership and, above all, transparency from both political leaders and civil society groups.

In Manipur, in the past years, the state's political leadership, cocooned in Imphal, seems to have abdicated its responsibility to ensure the first and abiding right of all citizens: to ensure their safety and enable them to live a 'normal' life. That appears to be the only logic which fuels its decision to arm villagers who wanted a respite from the extortion and intimidation of armed groups. As anyone who knows the situation would have predicted, the villagers have now become targets of the anger of these very groups and now require police and military protection. Armed with draconian laws, backed by the might of the Indian Army, paramilitary forces and its own state police, Manipur has declared its helplessness to protect its citizens. Instead it re-enacts the deadly farce of a Salwa Jhulum from Jharkhand, where villagers are armed against Naxalites, and suffer heavily at their hands. A government that proclaims its inability to protect its own people has no business to hold office.

Talk about normalcy in many parts of the North-east, and you'll probably get laughed at—that's the state of things at a time of disquiet. The use of anti-terror weaponry in the form of a major State assault or special laws is not a reflection of firmness or good governance. It actually shows up governments as running away, scared of such situations and unable to deal with the roots of these conflicts and angers. The result is a growing mess for themselves and trauma for others in the region.

There are times when a military response appears to be necessary. But once the immediate compulsion is over, this must be swiftly followed by political initiatives, which give power to those who can use it democratically and fearlessly. One reason for the continuing imbroglio over land and other issues in the Naga story is that the Government of India should have initiated discussions with the Naga leadership much earlier, as part of a process of getting them to understand the realities of the situation. One cannot solve problems, which are over fifty years old, which have resulted in thousands of deaths, alienated communities and created so much hurt and bitterness, in a few years.

The government is aware of that and has over these past

months been talking patiently on these issues, leading Thiungaleng Muivah, the general secretary of the National Socialist Council of Nagalim—the acronym (I-M) is derived from his name and that of his compatriot and organization chairman, Isak Chisi Swu—to publicly appreciate its position. But in the next breath, Muivah asserts that Nagas must live together as they have for centuries because they are not living in anyone else's territory but their own. It sounds extremely logical but is divorced from reality, at least for the time being, because none of the three states from where the 'traditional land of the Nagas' (Assam, Manipur and Arunachal Pradesh) is sought, is prepared to give an inch of territory.

The question then arises: where do the two negotiating parties go from here? Can there be an interim agreement which in general terms recognizes the fact that there are contending claims on land and empowers Nagas to vote, while staying within their own current states, for a Naga Council or Assembly? The latter could perhaps draw elected representatives from all states and act as a legally and constitutionally empowered group to secure the traditional interests of Nagas there, by interacting with their respective governments.

In addition, as a parallel process, could the traditional self-governing Naga institutions in all states, with better representation of women and other groups, be facilitated to run their own local affairs such as roads, courts, village development and agricultural extension, through direct funding from the Centre (as in the case of panchayats and district councils, this can be done through a specific budget line in the state budget which ensures that the funds go to these bodies)? Other features such as a flag for Nagaland, which could be flown next to the Indian tricolour, could be added.

There's a catch, though: how do you bring on board those groups which are opposed to the NSCN (I-M)? That is as challenging as dealing with the territorial issue and one possible way forward had been through the Reconciliation Commission comprising of church elders and the senior Naga leader, Niketu Iralu, the group's chairman. But that process fell through with the NSCN (I-M) repudiating the group, imputing motives to it and denouncing its chairman, who is one of the finest and most honourable human beings that I have known. Things have not made easier by the I-M leadership's ideologically tough line saying that reconciliation would have to sub-serve 'national goals' and the other factions would have to accept their mistakes. In other words, they have wanted the others to virtually fall at their feet and beg for forgiveness. That is unacceptable to the 'others,' who complain that they have been more sinned against than sinning.

The fact of the matter is that most Nagas view all Naga fighters, no matter to which group they belong, as 'national workers' and deserving of equal honour and merit. That point is being stressed by the activist groups and needs to be taken on board by the NSCN (I-M).

Many speak glibly of having something along the lines of the Truth and Reconciliation Commission (TRC) of South Africa for Nagaland and parts of the North-east. We would do well to remember that the TRC came after the dismantling of apartheid and the installation of Nelson Mandela as president.

We cannot have a mere duplication of that process: our conditions are different and perhaps even more complex. But some form of conciliation is clearly required and that is what a group of Naga church elders told Muivah and Swu in a marathon discussion at their camp near Dimapur, the commercial capital of Nagaland. The church group and others had denounced the rival faction for issuing a virtual death threat to members of the Tangkhul tribe and demanding that they quit Nagaland. However, what really irked the Naga leadership was a call by the Nagaland Baptist Church Council for Tangkhuls to speak out against intimidation and pressure. The response to this showed how deeply divided the Nagas remain, on ideological, organizational and even tribal lines

The Tangkhuls are the tribe of Muivah and they are predominantly located in Manipur's hills; however, groups of Tangkhul students and professionals, including government employees, live in Nagaland. Significantly, Tangkhuls dominate the NSCN (I-M) and many cadres are based in Dimapur, which represents the richest prize for the fighting groups—it is both cash cow, with extensive business and trade which pay protection money, and base.

*

At a workshop at Tufts University in the Boston area, one of the strongly debated topics was the whole concept of transitional justice. Broadly explained, this is about whether nations have a 'right' to inflict on a smaller country, a weaker population group or dissenting segment, their concept of what constitutes justice, or justify even violent actions to achieve results in their favour.

It's essentially a-winner-take-all scenario, where the victor does and can do no wrong. And, largely, this is a scenario that emerges in a country's post-independence era or after one in which a country has been dramatically reshaped by internal change and political events, such as the restructuring of the Soviet Union and the emergence of Russia.

Despite all of India's failings and shortcomings, the many laws which intimidate people and brutalize them, the acts of omission and commission by the State and its agencies, it inconceivable that a body like Parliament, or even a state legislature, would have accepted a situation like that which prevailed in Russia some years back where parliamentarians were basically shut up and shut out by the Government and its henchmen.

But how do we deal with issues that defy normal piecemeal solutions, some of which the Indian state is good at cobbling together? These are often ad hoc settlements that are not sustainable in character because while they may be good in law they frequently do not address the core of the issues.

Let us take the question of Nagaland and of the Naga demand, as reflected by the NSCN or National Socialist Council of Nagalim (as one group designates the land of Nagas), not for sovereignty but for Nagas to live 'under one administrative roof.'

Such a demand is understandable whether we like it or not. This has been a consistent demand of the Naga leadership, and in black and white, since the 1960s, the time of the Memorandum of Agreement between some Naga leaders and New Delhi, leading to the formation of the state. Not all the sixteen points in the Memorandum were agreed to by the then Prime Minister Jawaharlal Nehru, including this very demand (he suggested that discussions on the territorial issue be postponed to a later date—but he did not reject it out of hand). But the issue cannot be avoided, especially since the 1964 ceasefire (yes, there was one as far back as that!) between the Federal Government of Nagaland and New Delhi covered those hill districts of Manipur that the present Naga leadership wants in its 'Nagalim'.

It should be noted that the Federal Government of Nagaland was represented politically by the Naga National Council, which later split and led to the formation of two NSCNs, one under Thuingaleng Muivah and Isak Swu and the other under S.S. Khaplang. Talks were held at the level of the then prime minister, Indira Gandhi, and the issue fell under the jurisdiction of the Ministry of External Affairs before it was transferred to the Home Ministry. So there is a certain history that we cannot deny.

The Naga National Council (NNC) was the founder and leader of the Naga movement. But things changed after the Shillong Accord of 1975 between a section of the Naga underground and the Government of India. Under terrific pressure from the Indian Army and exhausted by attrition against the civil population, this group accepted the Indian Constitution, agreed to lay down their arms and work for a final settlement. That agreement confused the Naga public and fractured both the mandate and the movement.

But let us not just focus on this alone. These are weighty issues to be decided by our 'national' leadership (although little can be done without the clearance of the security-military apparatus) and the Naga 'collective' leadership of Muivah and Swu. However, there is a major catch—since the Nagas are not homogenous (there are sixteen tribes in Nagaland alone and about twice that number overall), the I-M faction has been fiercely challenged by the Khaplang group and more recently by a breakaway faction calling itself the Unification group, which after suffering heavy casualties in confrontations with its former mentor, merged with Khaplang. There have been gun battles and fights without number between the groups while the Indian Army remains in barracks and the local police mute spectators. Nagaland's government leaders farcically maintain that the fighting is not a 'law and order problem but a political problem'.

Granted that the Indian State is probably patronizing the Khaplang group and wants to extend the ceasefire ad infinitum while wearing down Muivah's group, the fighting raises an issue that cannot be glossed over—the internal, acute and abiding divisions among the Nagas. How are these to be overcome?

Can a peace or a peace accord last if there are such bitter divisions? How can these conflicts be reduced? Can there be a political settlement before reconciliation, assuming that the latter is required? Unless the two sides stop their conflicts, there is little hope of a long-term sustainable settlement. There is wisdom in what Nelson Mandela said to his old friend and comrade Mac Maharaj, about overcoming the desire to avenge decades of suffering— 'Let it go'. He was talking about letting go of bitterness, a powerful tool for destructive change in a wounded society that needed healing.

*

Naga leaders were fiercely opposed to the United Progressive Alliance coalition's Common Minimum Programme which declared that 'the territorial integrity of existing states will be maintained,' a reference to the Naga demand for integration of territories currently in Assam, Arunachal Pradesh and

Manipur, and wanted this clause removed. But they have been realistic enough not to insist on their demand and have restrained themselves to table-thumping and rhetoric.

While some Naga bodies maintain that this is setting conditions to the ongoing negotiations which are supposed to be 'unconditional', it is clear that whatever the public posturing of both sides, the NSCN (I-M) is focusing on integration and not on 'sovereignty' which many Nagas know is near-impossible. Where will the talks go if integration too is not possible, is their concern.

While understanding the concerns of the Nagas, who have an oral history and no structured form of unified government embracing their sixteen tribes, it is also important that Nagas understand the written history and chronicles of their neighbours, going back hundreds of years, especially Manipur and Assam. The Nagas are unique in the sense that they have kept up an armed struggle and consistent political position over the past fifty-odd years, in terms of their historical perspective.

But this is a world where ground realities matter as much as emotions and views. That reality is that borders were drawn decades ago, that states exist under a constitutional arrangement and these borders matter as much to the existing states and peoples as do the Naga demands to Nagas. Confidence-building measures are necessary among communities, to reduce tension and suspicion, involving scholars, policy-makers and analysts, media and non-government organizations. Without an understanding between peoples of the states, it will be difficult to push through an agreement.

After visits to the region and interactions with leaders on

all sides over a number of years, I propose the following formula for consideration by all sides to nudge the process forward:

One, that an expert committee, comprising of lawyers, government officials, demographers, scholars and former officials who are respected by all sides, be set up to consider the historical and contemporary situation with regard to communities living on either side of the existing borders and this group should submit its recommendations and report within a year and be assisted by all sides with a stake in the situation;

Two, that the team's recommendations be circulated and debated extensively, openly and vigorously and provided to the media; the report must be submitted to governments and relevant organizations for detailed discussions in a move toward a long-term settlement that would be based upon agreement if not consensus;

Three, that without prejudice to a political resolution of the issues, that the traditional residency of ethnic groups which have lived and co-existed in these areas for generations should be recognized. Conventions, conversations, detailed group discussions and dialogues at village levels covering these aspects by civil society groups, including the Church, could help bridge gaps and build understanding.

To me, these suggestions form the core of an open and democratic approach, the basis of a genuine dialogue among stakeholders that would involve the people and pave the way for a long-term settlement. Without such an involvement—as in economic planning and engineering— few government proposals and programmes, especially on such sensitive issues, can work. Governments which seek to move forward unilaterally, without such a participative approach, and try for a quick fix by talking to just one or two powerful groups, will create more trauma, pain and bloodshed. The cycle of nightmares will continue because it will then have been demonstrated that some stakeholders are disinterested in solutions; they only want to keep stirring the pot to ensure that their power prevails.

Let the Bloodshed End

Let the fur fly, let angry words be exchanged,, let emotions run high. Yet, words, however hurtful or disagreeable, are better than firing bullets, laying ambushes and creating fear and tension. Let the debate begin.

There are two moving memorials in Kohima and Khonoma in Nagaland that evoke a history of defiance and bravery. The first is well-known and lies at the foot of the Kohima War Cemetery maintained by the Commonwealth War Graves Commission in the state capital, built along the tennis courts of the Deputy Commissioner's bungalow. Kohima was where the Japanese forces in World War II were slowed, stalled and then pushed back by a band of determined British and Indian troops. The words on the high marble slab over the busy intersection in Kohima, attributed to John Maxwell Edmonds (1875–1958), are a strong reminder of the lives lost in this and countless other battles, on many fronts across the world:

When you go home, Tell Them of Us and Say,
For Their Tomorrow, We Gave Our Today

An hour's run from Kohima is the village of Khonoma, flanked by dappled, forested hillsides and terraced rice fields. A great stone church dominates the village, clinging on to one hilltop, while houses are built in a sprawl of wood, stone and cement, and run up and down the other slopes. Khonoma is about four hundred years old and is a major symbol of power and resistance for the Nagas — both against the British and India.

It is the home of the late Angami Zapu Phizo, who mobilized the Naga National Council and led the Federal Government of Nagaland (FGN), in its bitter armed campaign against New Delhi, asserting that the Nagas were not and would never be 'Indians'. And it was a Khonoma resident who is said to have walked to a telegraph office on 14 August 1947 in Kohima and sent a message out to the fledgling United Nations that the Nagas had declared Independence. This story, whether partly or wholly true, has found itself into Naga lore.

It is a village that suffered at the hands of the British and the Indian Army: both destroyed it at least once for its defiance. In the square, as one enters, is a simple stone block, painted in the blue and white 'national' colours of the Naga National Council (this flag of Naga independence is accepted by other rival armed groups) with the names of fifty-six men who died fighting for their village and their cause. It praises the 'heroes who died so that we may be free'. This is an extraordinary monument simply because it still exists. Where else can one find a greater tribute to co-existence and democracy—where the larger group accepts the right of the smaller to pledge defiance?

The negotiations that the Government of India have been conducting since 1997 with the main Naga militant group, the National Socialist Council of Nagalim (NSCN) of Isak Swu and Th. Muivah (I-M), needs to be seen in this spirit of mutual acceptance. India has a ceasefire but no negotiations with the other major Naga group led by S.S. Khaplang.

There is another aspect to Khonoma that needs to be taken note of: reconciliation has taken place between two major clans, divided for decades over a killing. This division lasted over forty years but finally, after years of dialogue and discussions, one elder took responsibility for the tragedy, apologized to the other family and called for healing. The apology was accepted and an old bitterness was finally buried.

It is this kind of reconciliation—at the individual, community, tribal and political level—that is crucial if political agreements at a higher level are to take place and bear fruit. Such a healing touch can cement the foundation of good politics and strong negotiations, although it cannot replace the latter.

This action is relevant to the current situation; it takes great courage to put the past behind and accept one's mistake. It should be noted that the acute differences between Muivah's group and that of Khaplang grew out of mutual suspicions, followed by a bloody assault by the latter's followers on a remote camp in Myanmar housing Muivah's fighters.

*

Despite these moves, there has been a new kid on the block, heavily armed and looking for a fight, the NSCN (Unification), comprising of dissidents in the I-M who were largely members of the Sema or Sumi tribe, the tribe of Isak Chisi Swu, the Chairman of the I-M group. Confusing? It doesn't get much easier because the I-M and Unification group engaged in furious attacks and counter-attacks in towns and villages in the summer of 2008, along roads and highways, in broad daylight, with the state and Central governments either helpless onlookers or complicit in the brutal violence that has erupted, in which scores have died. The U group then joined the Khaplang faction and there are fears in Nagaland that it was secretly backed by the Centre, aimed at weakening the I-M and its leadership. These concerns are fuelled by the realization that the rivalry is fracturing the state's already fragile peace and has led to an unravelling of the tension between various tribes, which in turn dominate the armed groups. There is support in Nagaland and elsewhere in the North-east for the suspicion that Delhi is 'behind' the fragmenting of the insurgent cause; after all, the Centre's security and intelligence agencies were behind the division in the ranks of the Federal Government of Nagaland and the Naga National Council in the 1960s, between Sema fighters and the Angamis, with accusations of betrayal being hurled against each other.

The Angamis are the tribe of Phizo who led the powerful upsurge against India and gave it ideological moorings, a cogent narrative and a national and international impact that resonates today.

In the Naga Hills, memories do not die along with those who bear them. Each generation appears to carry a stronger remembrance of pain inflicted on them by the 'other' by the retelling of these stories and experiences. The rivalries among armed groups and tribal communities appear, to an outsider, to have deepened and sharpened on the touchstone of hate and suspicion, despite the best efforts of reconcilers and the words and deeds of good men and women in the Church and outside.

*

The journey to Somdel, a village in Ukhrul district, dominated by the Tangkhul Nagas, was one that I had long wanted to make. The Tangkhuls are one of the most prominent and best educated of the Naga tribes, in Manipur and outside of it. They have provided some of the finest organizers and fighters of the Naga battle for separation from India. Somdel is to the Nagas of Manipur what Khonoma is to their people in neighbouring Nagaland: the home of their most influential leader, Thiungaleng Muivah, general secretary of the NSCN (I-M).

Muivah lived abroad for nearly thirty-eight years, since he led the equivalent of the Long March to China, along with General Thinsolie Keyho, over jungles and mountains through Myanmar into Yunnan Province in 1966 and established contact and gained support from the Chinese. That official backing ended in 1976. After a visit to Somdel a few years ago, I concluded that these hill tracts must have prepared Muivah for his legendary treks: there was no road, just a hill track on which no bus or truck could travel, barring the village jeep and the occasional army and police patrol.

Often, as one travels in such isolated parts of the Northeast, one realizes that what the Nagas and other groups have is de facto separation in such places. What they want is a legalized adaptation of that reality or de jure acceptance.

If there has to be movement forward out of the current log jam, the Government of India must call joint consultations with the chief ministers and top officials of the neighbouring states of Nagaland as well to brief them on the progress of the talks with the NSCN and seek their views. Such an exercise will make consultations more transparent. But in a democracy, there's always an election around the corner! And which government or political party is prepared to take decisions that could have repercussions on its electoral prospects?

So the talks will meander on, partly because it is difficult for the NSCN (I-M) to pull out. This suits New Delhi because no party to the talks can be seen as anti-peace.

The core of the discussions among representatives of the Centre and the NSCN revolves around three issues related to the Constitution: what is acceptable to both, what is not and what needs change. These are questions that are unlikely to be concluded in any haste.

Yet, although troops on either side are not confronting each other, the situation in Nagaland is still fraught with danger: the major rival groups, NSCN (I-M) and the NSCN (K) allied to the FGN cadres have been engaging each other in furious gunfights in district headquarters, smaller towns and elsewhere, creating panic and deep concern. Manipur is a case apart: the Nagas and Kukis have carved out spheres of influences for themselves in the hills ringing the Imphal Valley. The Meitei armed groups are influential in the Valley and the state faces internal collapse.

In Nagaland, the state government appears unable or unwilling to do anything on the issue, beyond saying that it is a 'political' problem. Take the riot that erupted in the Tangkhul colony in Dimapur, the largest town in Nagaland,. Hundreds of Tangkhul homes were gutted after a mob rampaged through the area, following a series of incidents involving the reported high-handedness of I-M cadres and Tangkhul youth. No Tangkhul was physically harmed but the homes of top leaders of the I-M were razed. That was an outburst of anger, which had been building up for some time, and it should be noted that the I-M leadership of Muivah and Swu were at their Hebron Camp, not far from Dimapur, at the time.

Ironically, years of negotiations with the Centre have seen a sharpening of the divide among Nagas, especially on ethnic and loyalist lines. The Church tries to reduce tension but finds itself rebuffed by both sides, each unwilling to trust the other.

What was once a bilateral issue between New Delhi and the Nagas has now become an internal matter of India. And this is angering other factions and an older generation who have seen many Naga 'national workers', as the armed and political cadres are called, die for the cause.

The NSCN (I-M) is not negotiating for the Naga right to sovereignty, although this has been at the heart of the struggle. Leaders of the I-M have proclaimed that even the US is not truly sovereign in a changing world.

The 'mother of all insurgencies', as I had once described the NSCN (I-M), too is no longer sovereign; it does not control the smaller groups. There are collaborations and contacts but armed factions in Assam, Tripura and, of course, Manipur, plough their own furrows.

The Naga negotiations at some point take on an air of unreality when we hear discussions about a 'federal relationship' between the Nagas and the Centre. This is a fine concept and some media pundits and scholars have enthusiastically applauded such a move. A relationship between the Nagas and the Centre cannot be seen independently of the relations between the Centre and other parts of the country. Of course, all states of the Union may be allowed to fly their own flag and sing their own state anthem, but is the Centre prepared to shed its enormous control to just running defence, finance, communications and foreign affairs? I doubt it: I am all for out-of-the-box thinking but there should be a practical understanding of the Centre's interest or lack of it in embracing changes.

One example should suffice: New Delhi is determined not to act on the recommendations of the Committee which reviewed the Armed Forces Special Powers Act and which proposed the repeal of this obnoxious law as far back as June 2005. How far will it go with the Nagas who are demanding not just parity but a separate entity that includes the carving up of three neighbouring states? (The Central government has not even made the AFSPA Review report public but it is in the public domain after the *Hindu* put it on its website).

*

There is another aspect to the Naga and North-east story. It is not insignificant that nearly a half century after Muivah's epic march to Yunnan, thousands of young Nagas, Mizos, Manipuris and Assamese are making another long trek—to better educational institutions in different parts of the country and even abroad, which lead to improved livelihoods, incomes and professions. Their worldview is changing and although convictions about their past run deep, there is lack of certainty about the future.

This represents another loss: the brain drain of some of the best and brightest from Nagaland and the North-east, fleeing the land they love but one which has morphed into a place where they do not seek a future. Those who can afford to are making this move in style, living in rented apartments, moving about in flashy motorbikes or cars. Others are doing it the hard way, with several young men or women sharing tiny flats, cooking for themselves and travelling long distances to study and work. Today, there are many North-eastern faces at malls and restaurants in Indian metros, among airline crews, the fashion industry and in media. This is both a sign of hope and of concern because there is a danger of stereotyping in some of these jobs, especially in the hospitality sector. The next years could be a transitory phase between location in the service lane and greater participation in professions and businesses.

Another tragic effect of decades of conflict is also visible: people are distancing themselves from the pain that is played out every day in their homes by going almost as far away as they can. Yet while doing so they are unable to severe all ties and thus remained buffeted by the very angst, turmoil and stress that they have fled. Studies among children and adults in Nagaland especially have turned up disturbing trends with extensive accounts of cases of Post-Traumatic Stress Syndrome (PTSS) and Post-Traumatic Stress Disorder (PTSD) which are results of regular exposure to violence.

Children and others surveyed were mentally disturbed, found themselves under acute stress and unable to relax, and in many cases slept poorly. Few have received professional counselling in conflict-ridden areas such as Nagaland, Manipur, Assam and Tripura. Women who have been raped and molested decades ago still bear mental scars of the horror; PTSS victims include children who have seen a parent or relative shot in front of their eyes, wives or mothers whose husbands or children have disappeared. The list is endless. Such problems are there in Mizoram, touted today as the country's most peaceful state which went through twenty years of insurgency and State repression and another twenty years of rebuilding. Without counselling and proper treatment, these nightmares do not go away; they may be buried but emerge from time to time to haunt the victim. This is the hidden cost of our internal conflicts, a price which has not been assessed because it is incalculable and continues to silently wound and bleed individuals and societies.

Bearing an Olive Branch

As he sipped at a Coke in an Amsterdam restaurant full of cigarette smoke and spoke with passion and conviction, Thiungaleng Muivah, one of the most remarkable political figures of post-colonial South Asia, declared that the military era in 'Indo-Naga relations' was over and described the current phase as a political era to settle the issue. Taking desultory bites at the hamburger before him, he ignored the hours that slipped by, and ranged over a broad canvas of regional and international issues.

As part of practical politics, he was clear that 'objective reality' determined 99 per cent of policy. This was the approach he and his colleague, Isak Chisi Swu of the NSCN (I-M), would take in settling the problem. In this conversation in February 2003, Muivah dismissed the criticism of his group by the Naga National Council of Ms Adinno Phizo, who is based in London, as of 'no consequence'. The NNC is accused of supporting the 1975 Shillong accord which divided the Naga movement and brought one group out of the underground. 'If some people think that the NNC and we should unite and become strong, that is not so—it is a foolish calculation and we will not fall for it.'

Governments talk to groups on the basis of their strength, he said. 'The Indians also have to be convinced about it,' he added, saying that the NSCN (I-M)'s armed and political strength had enabled it to withstand Indian pressure and force a major victory for the Nagas—an acknowledgment by New Delhi that the Naga issue was a political one and could not be resolved by military means. Muivah spent a considerable amount of time asserting why neither Khaplang nor the former chief minister of Nagaland, S.C. Jamir, could be trusted. Khaplang, he said, was responsible for the armed attack on his camps in western Myanmar, in 1988, in which over one hundred of his best cadres were killed but, miraculously, he and his wife escaped. He accused the Naga leader, who has also been based in Myanmar, of declaring that his main enemy was not India but the Muivah-Isak group. The bitterness runs deep and sharp: 'Can this be denied? Can he regret for this kind of mistake? He wants to bargain using the slogans of reconciliation and unity.'

Muivah also was critical of efforts to push reconciliation and unity by Naga civil society groups, accusing them of 'bias'. 'Peace and reconciliation cannot be forced, it has to come naturally,' said Muivah, his utterances laced with philosophical notes that underlined his approach to politics and dialogue. The most powerful of the Naga leaders was skeptical about mechanically replicating the truth and reconciliation commissions that had worked in South Africa when apartheid was being dismantled. The NSCN needed to be realistic to the extent that 'everyone can't be trusted. This is practical politics and to be realistic is better than to be good.'

But despite the issues that Muivah is unwilling to compromise on—and many civil society leaders regard such a tough position as hurtful to the overall peace process among the deeply divided Nagas—he has some positive things to say. Such as recognizing the 'reality of India 10 times more' if India understood the 'reality of the Nagas'; that neither can New Delhi crush the Nagas nor can the Nagas throw out a superior military force; that the Nagas will be the most reliable friend to India and that the present situation was 'the finest opportunity which should be seized with both hands'.

After saying this, Muivah addressed this writer as an 'Assamese' and said that while Assam and Manipur needed to be more sensitive to the Nagas—'If we don't understand each other, how will we solve the problem?'—he also urged the two states not to rush to Delhi for shelter and succour. Then came the brilliant punch line: he was prepared, Muivah said, to offer himself as a negotiator to calm the fears of the neighbours.

In one stroke, Muivah had tried to de-fang his detractors, for he knows how contentious the territorial issue is, and cast himself in the role of an elder statesman. This is a bold new gesture that could either complicate matters or, deftly sidestepping New Delhi, seek to deal directly with the states. Of course, it is unlikely that Assam, Manipur or Arunachal Pradesh will rise to this bait—but it is an expression of the remarkable diplomatic dexterity of the man, that he seeks to turn disadvantage to advantage, a difficulty into an asset. It is a characteristic that has stood him well since the 1960s. Think of the exquisite irony: here is one of the most criticized figures of the North-east, certainly of Manipur, offering an olive branch to his detractors. And he underlines his determination: 'Nagas cannot ignore the reality of Assam. If Nagas do that it is a mistake. We respect that reality. We have to accept that and I can prepare myself for talks. We will respect the Manipuris. Will the Manipuris respect the Nagas?'

However, one question remains for Muivah—can he also rise above his principled and personal opposition to men like Khaplang and Jamir and emerge as the statesman that all Nagas are looking for? That is a question only he can answer.

*

Muivah sets the pace for negotiations; others follow him. This is worth pondering, especially in the absence of an influential and equally articulate and skilled second rung of leadership within the organization that could eventually take over from him and NSCN Chairman Swu.

When I visited him at the sprawling Government safe house where he and his team were located in New Delhi during a marathon visit and marathon negotiations (which did not move the process forward much), he appreciated the *gamosa*, the hand-woven cotton embroidered scarf, a traditional Assamese form of greeting, that I had brought for him. And he was open in his conversations, blunt but fair, over sips of his favourite jasmine tea. Physically he had changed little over the years; perhaps he was a bit heavier but otherwise he looked much the same as he did at our first meeting in Bangkok several years ago.

In the unending negotiations with the Centre, Muivah heads a team which has held talks with a three-member Group of Ministers led by Union Minister Oscar Fernandes and assisted by former Home Secretary, K. Padmanabhiah, who, despite criticism of his role, has persistently carried on with the negotiations and ensured they never stalled, even if they did run into foul weather regularly (in the process he's picked up a Padma Bhushan, one of the country's highest civilian awards for meritorious service).

Muivah has known that it's going to be a long haul, given the sensitivity of the issue and the number of stakeholders and interested parties back home. He's prepared to be patient but that should not be construed as weakness. Yet, the Nagas now find themselves holding the sharp end of the stick, they are really between a rock and a hard place because the Centre will neither concede their demand for sovereignty nor redraw the borders of the North-east to give them a greater Nagaland or Nagalim, fearing emotional outrage and a political explosion even in Congress-run states like Assam, Manipur and Arunachal Pradesh which do not wish to part with an inch of territory.

Land, as we have seen elsewhere in this book, is a prickly, powerful issue that defines ethnic boundaries, social tensions, government functionality and a range of emotions, swinging from anger and bitterness to fear and loathing, across the entire region but especially in Assam and Manipur.

Like his physical appearance, Muivah's basic political stance has changed little: there appears to be little or no compromise in his view that Naga lands must be restored to his people, referring to the forests and lands which were 'taken away' by the British and placed in Assam and the drawing of state borders by the latter and by New Delhi. He

---

* Under Art. 3 of the Constitution, the Centre can create new states and draw fresh boundaries unilaterally without a reference to the states. But it knows it cannot do so in the case of the Naga demand without triggering a furious and violent reaction in Assam, Manipur and Arunachal Pradesh

blames Jawaharlal Nehru for much of the present mess and the initial confrontation with the Nagas which has cost both sides dearly.

There is a familiarity about the rhetoric and remarks. But what is new is his readiness to reach out and hold conversations with other sides or interested parties in the issues. He believes that justice, honour and history are on the Naga side, and that political goals and slogans must be tempered with realism. This is a side of Muivah which has not come across strongly enough in other media and political groups in the region, which have portrayed him as unbending and unresponsive to the histories of others. He spoke of the need to recognize that the people of the region were neighbours, that they had a shared destiny and no solution could be forced upon others.

In fact, at a 'consultative' meeting with Naga civil society leaders in Bangkok in 2002, Muivah had personally intervened to insert a clause in the final declaration which said that the Nagas must allay the 'apprehensions' of their neighbours. There are thus two sides to his approach—one is the familiar firm unbending resolve to get his way and the other is a lesser visible willingness which recognizes the need to reach out. Often the former gets the better of the latter. One of the last living legends of the Asian theatre of insurgency, Muivah has travelled the world, unfurling the Naga banner at different forums.

One undeniable achievement is to take the Naga issue for discussion to the level of the head of the Government of India, without conditions. It has moved from a third country outside India to this long, drawn-out and possibly final phase of negotiations in New Delhi. The scale of this achievement should be evident when we note that in places like Jammu and Kashmir, leave aside the North-east, other insurgent groups haven't even reached the first stage.

The talks have not been smooth sailing. Whenever either side has placed conditions, negotiations have floundered. The United Progressive Alliance of Prime Minister Manmohan Singh and Congress President Sonia Gandhi stands for the integrity of the boundaries of the North-eastern states; this is a problem but not necessarily unsurpassable, even though Muivah and his team see it as a stumbling block.*

Negotiators avoid the hurdle. When one issue did erupt fiercely—the extension of the ceasefire to other parts of the region in 2001, a move that led to riots in the Imphal Valley in Manipur and an exodus of Nagas from the Valley to the hills—there was enough realism on either side to see that this could hurt long-term goals. New Delhi withdrew the statement, although it was something to which it had been committed in earlier rounds of talks! Clearly, the Centre had been unprepared for the volatile response from the Meiteis of Manipur. The ceasefire extension has not become a sticking point; it remains an undercurrent and there is a tacit ceasefire in those other geographical areas where Nagas dominate, especially in the northern hills of Manipur and parts of Arunachal Pradesh, abutting Nagaland.

The Government of India must facilitate Muivah's meetings with other groups in the neighbourhood, to hear other voices which do not agree with him and can share a different perspective, without being dogmatic. Conversations with Muivah reinforce these views. Bridges of understanding must be built within the region if peace is to be cemented. But time, as always, is the problem. With each passing day, and new players emerging, the Naga situation is becoming more complex with a cast of characters which are supported by insurgent groups as well as various security and intelligence agencies of almost every government organization, seeking to pull each other down and jousting for space and a place of power in the near future. Perhaps the Centre is not really interested in a solution but wants to manage the situation so that the principal parties in the process are constantly battling each other, losing sight of their original goals and possible solutions, weakening each other and benefitting only one player: New Delhi. This is one of the principal causes of disquiet because it is a game that the Indian State is familiar with and has played long, both as adept and bungler. The consequences are greater division among the Nagas, a growing frustration and bitterness among the public for being continuously marginalized and taken for granted by all sides (the ordinary people are the worst sufferers in such conflicts) and alienation both from the fighting groups as well as from the idea of India.

It is a different matter that thousands of young Nagas and others from the region are travelling to the giant metros of the country, each large enough to absorb the entire populations of some of the hill states, to seek education, jobs and make a new life away from the strife.

Assam as the End Loser of Violence

For weeks, protesters had blocked the national highway at Doom Dooma, among the major tea-producing areas of Tinsukia district. Their grievance appeared genuine: demanding justice for the family of a young man who was killed by the Army in the area, a man from the Moran community, one of the most economically-backward groups in Assam, which anyway is at the bottom of India's economic pile.

Members of the Morans and another indigenous group in Upper Assam, the Muttocks, (whose best known leader is Paresh Baruah, the commander of the armed cadres of the banned ULFA, who is heard, through his telephone conversations with media, supporters and others, but unseen since so few in the region have met him in recent years) are among those communities that have been supportive of anti-government movements in Assam, especially the campaigns against New Delhi. They have produced numerous cadres and leaders for ULFA, some of whom have also been killed over the years. In addition, there has been a steady attrition in the number of ordinary people who have died at the hands of security forces, both central and state.

So the pendulum of public opinion, anchored by a noisy and breathless media, has been swinging from the side of the militants on the run to the government and then back again, depending on the nature of conditions and the incidents which take place. Thus, when the ceasefire collapsed in September 2006 between ULFA and the Centre following the breakdown of talks between the ULFA-appointed delegation and New Delhi, the Army went after the armed faction. Public opinion was sharply divided, thinking the government had not done enough to bring the group to the negotiating table.

There was also confusion spawned by self-righteous members of the ULFA delegation and their acolytes in a new group called the People's Committee for Peace Initiatives in Assam (PCPIA). These groups in their myriad forms, claiming to speak on behalf of the people of Assam, have created confusion and divided people on ethnic and language lines.

ULFA has exploded bombs in public places to exhibit its ability to strike and also affirm its slide into an organization that uses terrorist methods, using funds sucked from Assam and supported by, according to security analysts, the Inter-Services Intelligence (ISI) and Bangladesh's Directorate General of Forces Intelligence (DGFI). Paresh Baruah's worth was estimated at $115 million by an international security assessment firm based in the United States, with business operations in India, Bangladesh, and Thailand and across South Asia.

ULFA's bombs and bullets kept killing ordinary people repeatedly, especially Hindi-speakers, in early 2007. The incidents drew public opprobrium and the government went after ULFA with a heavy hand. Although it appears that the Army is at times still groping, it has exerted major pressure on the organization. Many cadres have been killed, captured or have surrendered. This has depleted the active armed strength of the organization in Upper Assam.

The deaths are tragic. These were young Assamese who died for a cause that they did not understand, whose leaders they rarely, if ever, met and who could have had a fuller life. All of us, not just their families, have suffered a loss. All sides are to blame for this tragedy, for their inability to come to a coherent and realistic resolution of issues.

Many cadres have scattered to the fringes of Arunachal Pradesh and moved into Myanmar. Their contacts are at work, exploiting the anger of marginalized groups, and egging them on to confront the administration.

The Army, of course, plays into insurgent hands with unfailing regularity by picking up and killing people on suspicion, undoing the 'gains' they speak of with such vehemence. After one such incident, the Morans and Muttocks, at the instigation of ULFA and its front groups, launched a blockade of the district administration and then the national highway, shouting slogans against the Army and the government. The blockade raised tensions, fuelling hunger and anger in the areas beyond Doom Dooma as well as in neighbouring Arunachal Pradesh, since it was stopping food and fuel from reaching markets and homes, and led to a full-fledged crisis.

Doom Dooma is an old ULFA stronghold and a cash cow where extortion is common. The tea garden workers in the area were getting restive; the warning signals were out but the agitators were in no mood to relent. The denouement was not long in coming.

The agitators refused to let essential commodities go, despite official requests, demanding that the chief minister come personally to listen to their grievances. Finally, hundreds of tea garden workers, people slow to anger but once infuriated difficult to control, armed with bows and arrows, attacked the protesters, many of whom fled although others resisted. By nightfall, officials said, the demonstrators were asking for police and army protection and many were kept in a field under army protection before being dropped to their homes under police escort.

Who has won from such a confrontation, although the government crowed with glee? In the process, Assam has been harmed. The results are increasing inter-group bitterness, suspicion and violence.

Political issues need negotiation but these incidents—the death of ordinary people at the hands of security forces and the subsequent violence—only reduce the space for discussion.

*

The time of horror of the slaughter of Hindi-speakers in Assam by ULFA appears distant after the successful holding of the National Games in Guwahati in 2007 when the organization had first called for a boycott of the Games and then withdrew the call in the face of growing public frustration; Assam appeared upset at an opportunity to showcase its capacity being ruined and its reputation besmirched as a place known for hospitality and dignity.

Since about 2006, ULFA has morphed from an insurgent group to an organization that justifies the killing of innocents and the poor and yet claiming that it represents the 'people' of Assam, who have never voted for it or whose views have never been ascertained in any independent survey.

It is worth recalling ULFA's own contradictory statements.

For instance, take the one issued after the killings of Hindi-speakers, mostly settlers from Bihar, in Tinsukia, Dibrugarh and Dhemaji districts in Upper Assam. First it took responsibility and said it was avenging the Bihar Regiment's gunning down five of its cadres in Tinsukia's rural areas. Later in the same statement, it claimed that the government made ULFA the scapegoat for such incidents.

But let us return to the January 2007 killings, which began as suddenly and irrationally as they ended. There was little easing of Army pressure. The fear factor among ordinary people remains dominant in the isolated pockets where victims were targetted. To reduce this fear, as I have argued elsewhere, human security can be assured only through a semblance of governance but never without communications and connectivity. The Defence Ministry and the intelligence wings of the Central and state governments will oppose my view but what is needed is new technology in the form of mobile phones and towers to connect those living on islands and isolated pockets where roads and bridges cannot go. Phone calls can and will save lives not just from bullets but make a difference to the livelihoods and health of communities—connecting farmers to markets, the sick to medical help just to name two aspects.

*

The State needs also to remember that as ordinary people continue to be harassed, hurt or hit by security forces, doing what they say is their duty, that fickle creature called public opinion can turn against government. After all, this is the fourth major military operation against ULFA since the 1990s.

We need, occasionally to be reminded of events which have not become history yet which many either do not remember or prefer not to.

In 1991, Lt. Gen. Ajai Singh, who later became Governor of Assam and was then General Officer Commanding of the Tezpur-based Fourth Corps, led a riposte which devastated ULFA, forced it to talks in 1992 in New Delhi and even brought acceptance of the Indian Constitution from its chairman, Arobindo Rajkhowa, in New Delhi.

This arrangement fell through because of the refusal of Paresh Baruah, ULFA's army chief, to agree to it and the lack of political will in Delhi and Assam to push through a settlement. These events led to Baruah's ascendancy as well as that of the military wing in ULFA, besides enhancing the influence of the Inter-Services Intelligence (ISI) and Bangladesh's Directorate General of Field Intelligence (DGFI).

It is in this context that the dumbing down of issues by the media represents a broader failure to understand the many problems that beset the region, not just Assam. The media and its managers ensure that only part of a complex and difficult picture is painted for most readers, viewers or listeners (depending on the media of choice).

Thus, the military option can be used to create the political space for talks because only that will lead to a long-term solution. For talks to be meaningful, unlike in the past, they will have to be direct. As important is the fact that New Delhi and Dispur must be clear on their approach and goals. ULFA must be represented by decision-makers in the organization, not those who wait for phone calls to understand what steps are to be taken. The release of the five ULFA leaders that the group is seeking may be considered but only after it stops its violence and agrees to talks in India. Its leaders need to realize that they no longer have extensive public support. They are also running out of time.

*

In 2004, over a dozen Assamese schoolchildren and others at the Independence Day rally were killed in Dhemaji in a cold-blooded, premeditated bomb blast; it triggered unprecedented public and media fury against ULFA. The bitterness and anger of a generally mild people exploded. If this was an effort at asserting its firepower, it went terribly wrong. Even those in the media who sing ULFA's praises—in Assam and outside—had no choice but to fall in line with the general outrage. ULFA's bluff and bluster, its violent pursuit of an unachievable goal ('independence'), its abuse of those who wish an end to the violence had been exposed as never before.

The families of this group's leaders should repeatedly call on them to return to society—and face the consequences of their actions. If those schoolchildren had been their kin, how would they have reacted?

Perhaps only once in the past had there been a groundswell of public anger against this armed outfit and that during the kidnapping and murder of Sanjoy Ghose, the non-government development activist, on the island of Majuli in 1996. But that was mild compared to what happened after Dhemaji.

There are many roads, straight or winding, to peace processes; there are many steps to peace platforms; there are many sizes of negotiating rooms and conference tables. It is not necessary that one size or one room should fit all. What would work for the Nagas may not work for ULFA. What matters is that conversations should begin.

It is my view that both sides should indicate their willingness to talk openly, on all issues (without specifying any one and thus avoiding the bind of conditionality). ULFA would be surprised at how much goodwill it could still generate from such a move; it would not be seen as a step back or a surrender of its position but a display of political maturity which has been lacking. It would also send the right signal to potential investors and business and industry already in the region that the paths to peace would improve the road to development and economic growth.

*

In 1979, a group of young idealistic men had gathered in Sibsagar's Rang Ghar to set up ULFA, but idealism has gone by the wayside these days. The young men have moved into middle age, are living in other countries and, at least ULFA's leaders, enjoy considerable comfort, setting up businesses and continuing their violent activities. ULFA has become intolerant of those who disagree; its leaders appear to have lost touch with reality.

ULFA's cause has taken the lives of many of courageous young men and women who did not know what they were fighting for. Heaven knows, the State is responsible for many wrongs, rapes and custodial deaths, fake encounters, disappearances and other illegalities in Assam and other parts of India. But that does not and cannot justify what some armed groups have done.

With all the money that they have gathered, ULFA could have helped with regular flood relief efforts and saving lives in the Brahmaputra Valley, which repeatedly faces acute floods. They could have contributed from their funds to sympathetic individuals and organizations in cash and kind.

What 'freedom' does ULFA really want? Is it the same as people in the state want? That is freedom from fear, want, the lack of basic needs, insecurity and ill-health. There have been so many opportunities to listen to what people want—the elections have banished public fear and drawn the highest percentage of polling in India, time and again. People have brushed aside boycott calls. What is needed is an understanding that there is fatigue with the violence and the attrition it inflicts on individuals and societies —people want to live in peace, earn a decent living, put their children through school and college, give them a chance to compete in an increasingly competitive and globalized world and not live in fear and anger.

Whether the 'ceasefire' called by units of the influential 28th Battalion in the middle of 2008 will lead to an actual peace—the effort has been scorned by the leaders based in Bangladesh and some who remain in jail, facing various charges—is questionable. The economic interventions that the state government is pushing in old ULFA strongholds like Kakopathar in Tinsukia district are significant. Yet, neither these nor the relentless military pressure that forced the 28th Battalion to sue for peace will create a lasting peace, unless the political and military leadership of the organization also recognizes the fatigue with conflict and starts negotiations. The Central and State governments would need to keep the doors—and windows—open at all times.

The impact of decades of State and non-State violence in Assam and the North-east has taken a high toll of lives but also of image, business, growth, livelihoods and incomes. People are worse off today than they were ten years ago; we are at the bottom of India's economic heap, despite the enormous amount of funds pumped into the region. Do those who govern the state and those who rule from Delhi, as well as those who claim to speak in the name of Assam and other parts of the region, want the continuing suffering of the innocent, poor and marginalized while battles for greater political and security goals are played out?

Distant Neighbours

A Dyak woman and her child perched precariously on the running board... [illegible] ...

A burst of colour and fragrant flowers at the morning market in Namphalong, Myanmar, across the border from Moreh in Manipur.

Refugees, Exiles and Migrants

The history of the world has been marked by migration. Many of our ancestors came from elsewhere and are settled in some other place; people, like water, tend to find their own levels. Sometimes you have governments, such as in Indonesia, which resort to demographic engineering, for example in Irian Jaya. The Government used financial and land incentives to send people from the main island group of Java and Sumatra, to assert their control as a majority over smaller rebellious groups.

There are many kinds of migration—you have the acute onset movements with the possibility of return, which means migration forced by flash floods, or natural catastrophes like an earthquake of large magnitude. You can have an acute onset movement without the possibility of return. This means armed conflicts, man-made interventions, leading to the flight of refugees. Unless the violence ceases, there can be no resolution of the refugee issue.

You may have a slow onset movement with the possibility of return, like in the case of Tripura state in the North-east, on the Bangladesh border. Many people come for daily wage labour or for seasonal work and then they go back. And you have a slow onset movement with predictability but no possibility of return. This is really one of the most relevant factors to our ongoing work because it covers issues such as lack of employment locally and better chances of livelihood away from home, better health care and economic benefits in the receiving country. The fifth and last, is the slow onset movement without the possibility of return because of conditions in the migrant-producing areas, whether it is the Sahel and the Horn of Africa, or Bangladesh, or Myanmar, or Latin America, all witness to natural environmental changes: desertification, soil degradation/erosion, coastal flooding resulting from climatic changes and sea- level changes.

Some of these problems are irreversible. This is a fact of geography, of history, of the contemporary world. They can be curbed or mitigated through international multilateral assistance for adjustment and permanent settlement, but not prevented. Some years ago at an international conference in Geneva which was organized by the UNHCR and the International Organization for Migration (IOM), I had suggested that the international community should consider compensation for countries which are essentially receiving migrants—countries like India whose infrastructure and other facilities are under heavy strain anyway. It received some interest but nothing has happened. But across the world, we find concern is growing over the issues of migration, which is forced or created by economic pressures of landlessness, unemployment, of diminishing soil fertility as well as the failure of the State in the migrant-producing area to provide economic security to its people.

Myron Weiner, the late political scientist, further categorized the movement of people into two groups; one was Unwanted Migrants and the other was Rejected Peoples.

Under Unwanted Migrants you have the people who are not liked by the host community, whether it is the Bangladeshis who come to Assam and Meghalaya or the Madhesis, the people of Indian origin, who have settled in Nepal. As far as refugees are concerned, this group would come under the second category, which Weiner defined as Rejected Peoples. In this description, the classical refugees of our times are the Tibetans, the Kurds of Iraq and Turkey, the Tamils of Sri Lanka, the Afghans, including those who live in this country, the Chakmas of the Chittagong Hill Tracts, Bangladesh, and the Rohingyas of the Arakan in Myanmar. These are people who have been rejected by their own governments and fled oppression as in the case of the Tibetans.

A migrant is not necessarily a refugee. If one is speaking in economic or ecological terms, you have ecological and environmental migrants. 'Refugee' remains a political term. Yet a refugee can be a migrant. In many discussions, there is really a lot of confusion on this issue because an international migrant is not forcibly evicted or displaced. He/she chooses to move. It is a matter of personal choice and the attraction is better life in the new homeland. Take the case of India and Bangladesh. There is a 4,000-kilometre long border with West Bengal, Assam, Meghalaya and Tripura, of which about 800 kilometres in Meghalaya, 200 kilometres in Assam and 600 in West Bengal, are fenced. A cursory look at the map of the region, and Bangladesh's own statistics, will tell only a part of the story, though it is surely one of the defining conditions behind the situation. In the area, which now constitutes Bangladesh, the population doubled from 1961 to 1991, from 55 million to 111.4 million, and the latest data indicates a population of about 120 million. The density of 1,250 persons per sq km makes Bangladesh the most densely-populated country in the world. The pressure on land is acute and we are aware that substantial numbers are coming to India.

But why do people move? They don't pack their bags overnight and say that they will go to Dimapur or Mumbai or Guwahati or Delhi. They move out of desperation. In fact, a prominent Bangladesh academic has described it as a strategy of survival. I don't think it is a great conspiracy to overwhelm parts of India, although small groups which have a criminal intent or a terrorist aim can also infiltrate across borders, or be made to infiltrate the large numbers which are already moving. The Bangladesh Government continues to deny that there is any such movement, but from interactions with Bangladesh academics and others, including policy makers, there is a growing acknowledgement that this movement is taking place and it is beginning to be quite openly spoken about and studied there as well. The movement in Assam against illegal migration, which began in 1979, spread to other parts of the North-east in the 1980s. The reaction in West Bengal has not been as acute to the problem although it exists. But it is in the heart of the North- east, the Brahmaputra Valley, that the issue has been most visible, in terms of the scale of confrontation.

Obviously, the attractions of movement to lower population density areas are strong. We also need to look at the scale of flooding in Bangladesh itself. According to the Jehangir Nagar University, eighteen to twenty million people every year are displaced internally by floods and river bank erosion in Bangladesh. Obviously, not all displacees are coming to India, but it would not be implausible to believe that some of them do. The inherent law of migration is that people do not necessarily move long distances, they move to areas close to their homes, which are compatible, geographically and culturally. Over a period of time, this outflow can cross international borders. In the case of Assam there was organized settlement in the 1930s and 1940s, especially with the Muslim League in power. At that point India was one country, so it was not really illegal. But since then and post-Partition, the movement has been largely voluntary, apart from the initial years after Partition.

The Assam census report of 1931 spoke of how an entire population from East Bengal has transplanted itself 'in the last 25 years'. The then Census Commissioner said in a passage that is the favourite of the anti-immigrant lobby, 'I can compare it only to the mass movement of a huge body of ants'. Interestingly enough, although this was supported and organized by the Muslim League government in Assam at the time, the party which opposed it most strongly was the Congress. The Assamese position, in fact, angered leaders like Jawaharlal Nehru and Vallabhbhai Patel because they felt it was holding up the process of independence. Ultimately, Gandhiji sided with Assam. His support to the then Assam Premier, Gopinath Bardoloi, and his colleagues carried the day and blocked the British Government's plan to hive off Assam from India and join it to East Pakistan, an idea that had much support in the Muslim League and the pro-Pakistan lobby. This concern continues to trouble Assam even today.

The Assam agitation of the 1980s, led by student leaders who declared that 'local' people were in danger of being swamped by illegals and that this was both a demographic as well as social and political threat to Assam and the North-east, resulted in a major movement against outsiders. One spillover was the extensive ethnic, linguistic and religious clashes between the indigenous and the 'migrants' and widespread killings in 1983. In one area alone, in and around the sleepy little one-stop town of Nellie, bisected by a national highway, not less than 1,753 people were killed, overtly over land issues. All of those killed were Muslims of Bengali origin. Some of them were new settlers but many of them were old ones and were killed by mobs which included their neighbours; the killings were led by a group which had been planning it for weeks.

The immigrants, who were almost 100 per cent Muslims, had taken over land belonging to the Tiwa tribals, original inhabitants of the area, illegally by getting a 'chappa' (or thumb impression on pieces of paper) since this was an area where sale of tribal land was barred. The agitation and the elections of 1983 seemed like an opportunity to wrest the land back.

*

According to the Bangladeshi scholar, Meghna Guha-Thakurta, a review of population growth in her country turns up approximately 5 million missing Hindus. The Hindu population has grown by a bare 2 million in forty years, from 9.2 million in 1951 to 11.1 million in 1991, which is impossible. The Hindu rate of growth is pegged at 2.4 per cent; and there are a large number of people who are missing. And where would they go? They have not become converts, nor have they just vanished. They have essentially moved to what would be regarded as the 'homeland' over there, which are

West Bengal, Assam and Tripura.

It is not my argument that only one religious group is moving. The demographic changes in the border districts of West Bengal and Assam, and, to some extent, the changes in Meghalaya, are a clear indication of this. Indeed, the 2001 census shows a rise in density from 286 to 339 per sq km in Assam.

As for those Hindus from Bangladesh who have been the victims of religious and political violence, they are true refugees, they are not migrants. They are as traumatized, frightened and brutalized as refugees in any other part of the world. They have been targetted during successive national elections, particularly by thugs from the Bangladesh Nationalist Party of Begum Khaleda Zia, who have raped and pillaged and also seized Hindu properties. The attacks may have abated and the exodus has eased, but these incidents show the uncertainty and insecurity which remains a part of their lives, forcing people especially from the rural middle class and the marginalized to flee. But many Hindu professionals in Bangladesh continue to stay because of their privileges and positions, although they too feel economically and politically insecure. Most vulnerable are the small communities which live in small pockets surrounded by large majoritarian groups.

Many issues have been discussed detailing the conflict zones being created by illegal migration, not just from Bangladesh but elsewhere, but we also need to look at where we have failed to address the issue. For decades, we have spoken on the same issue in forum after forum, on the streets of Assam, in the media, and at policy levels, but little has happened. However, there is a major plus: there is a national consciousness, the issue is seen as a national problem and that is largely a tribute to the leadership of the All Assam Students Union. Today virtually every regional and national party has been forced to take a position on migration and that is no mean achievement. But the problem persists. In all these years, we have not been able to develop a calibrated response, based on rationality and reality. We still have people talking in the same terms as at the time of the students' agitation in the early 1980s—detection and deportation. We still don't know how many people have actually come across although often the talk is in terms of crores. At the peak of the Assam agitation, some spoke of two crore illegal migrants in the North-east. Almost twenty-five years later, the entire population in the North-east, according to the 2001 census, is 40 million i.e. four crores! Surely it is not anyone's argument that a majority of this population is made up of 'foreigners'. The idea is absurd.

That is why we must guard against rhetoric because it always misleads; it is divorced from reality. The Asom Gana Parishad, the AASU and the BJP have been speaking about the issues of illegal migration and threats to national security, potential violence and the local people being marginalized and outsiders taking political and economic control. We should be extremely careful when we use the word 'Bangladeshi' because it is becoming a pejorative word. Anybody who has been here since 1971 is a Bangladeshi. Those who have come before then are not, because there was no Bangladesh; they are from East Pakistan, which no longer exists. We need to look at issues in very practical terms because we must stop talking in the same monologue, in the same fashion, in the same dialectic, with the same flourishes which have characterized the issue since it came into the public eye. What has been the result of these agitations? Take Assam where the whole thing began. The Congress Party has come to power twice since 2001 partly because voters are no longer enthused by the chant of 'illegal migration.' Those elected to power on the basis of throwing out 'Bangladeshis', have either not been able to do anything about it or made a mess of it. New Delhi's reluctance, whether under the BJP or the Congress, to pursue the issue has sustained the problem of illegal migrants.

If this problem is to be tackled, we should look at issues specifically and not take a broad-brush approach. We must continue to fight for a logical approach to migration, based on facts not feelings. Policies need to cut across political parties, whatever their points of view on the subject.

The Asom Gana Parishad and the Bharatiya Janata Party as well as the Shiv Sena have it as one of their mantras during election time. But the Congress, though its younger leaders and members of state legislatures and Parliament see this is a sensitive and difficult issue, tends to follow the old ostrich approach, with the party reluctant to alienate its minority supporters, the Muslims. Yet, developments in Assam show disenchantment among this one-time solid vote bank. In the 2006 state assembly elections, Congress candidates lost to the supporters of a Muslim perfume business baron from the little town of Hojai in Central Assam. The latter captured no less than eleven seats, a striking performance for a new party. The BJP won the same number of seats and the AGP a handful more. Clearly, Congress has much to be concerned about and it is trying to win back its constituency and retain its pro-Muslim position by reaffirming that minorities will not be harassed in the name of detecting illegals.

It is worth remembering that the issue of migration in a Danish election changed a national government. Even President Andre Sarkosky's victory in France shows the resonance of the migration mantra and the pressure it exerts on 'traditional' societies and local infrastructure.

Another need is for a National Immigration Council or a National Immigration Commission because there are numerous solutions to this problem. We can talk about a law and order approach, a security approach, a legal approach, an NGO/human rights approach, but we do not have a mechanism that will enable us to look at the macro picture and break it up into smaller, manageable slices.

If there is a National Immigration Commission, as exists in the United States, we would be able to take a comprehensive look at the laws. For over twenty years, a prejudiced law existed which was applicable only to Assam: the Illegal Migrants (Determination by Tribunals) Act, which stood all laws on migrants and illegal entry on their head— it sought to force the complainant to prove the illegality of the person being complained against. This is the reverse of what exists across the world and is accepted universally as appropriate and just legal procedure. Naturally, prosecutions were few, although complaints were many (nearly 300,000), and convictions even fewer. The Supreme Court tossed that law out as well as another existent and hastily amended Foreigners Act which again sought to underline the difference between Assam and the rest of India—in plain language it stated that there would be one law for the rest of India but because of Assam's peculiar status, it would have to suffer another law, which tried to bring the IMDT through the back door. This too, to its credit, the Supreme Court tossed out.

Apart from migration legislation, we need to look at the related existing laws including the Foreigners' Act and the Citizenship Act. Perhaps the possibility of a National Migration Law and a National Refugee Law should be considered. We do not know how many refugees exist in this country. How many, for example, have come from Bhutan, escaping a crackdown on ethnic Nepalese and taken refuge in Kokrajhar and Darrang in Assam en route to Eastern Nepal? The numbers of Tibetans and Sri Lankan refugees are known. But not the numbers of Chins from Myanmar (Burma) and other ethnic groups there, who have come in a steady trickle since that country went under the heel of a brutal military regime in 1988. Estimates vary—exiles say there are up to 80,000 refugees in tiny Mizoram state, which has the largest number of Chin settlers. Independent scholars, media specialists and officials in Mizoram state say there are only about 200 refugees and political exiles; the rest are economic migrants who have fled economic hardship caused by irrational policies.

How do the security aspects tie in here? We should not make the mistake of thinking that barbed wire fences will protect our country. They cannot; they can be a tool in effective management and policing of the borders, but these are best guarded with the participation of and involvement of communities who live there, are acutely aware of the problem and by supporting the paramilitary Border Security Force with local police. It is the local police who know of the human smuggling routes and who is organizing them.

The BSF, good as it may be, is stymied by either lack of intelligence or the problem of non-cooperation. This is where new technology can help, with satellite mapping that enables authorities and those interested to see the movement of boats and vehicles, groups of people and individuals, although this is not fool-proof or fail-safe. If there is an illegal population of even 15–20 lakh (1.5–2 million) in Assam, it is unlikely that any state or national government will muster the courage, the strategy or the physical force to identify them, let alone turf them out.

The Jaipur bomb blasts of May 2008 underlined this issue: a hunt against 'Bangladeshis' was launched in that city and other places across India, although most of those rounded up were the poorest of society—rag pickers and labourers, giving the impression that the State was comfortable with locking up the poor and dispossessed if they did not have proper papers. In addition, the Home Ministry's proposal to set up internment camps for Bangladeshis, an idea which it has circulated to the States, is one of the most short-sighted and hair-brained schemes that a Central ministry, which is supposed to handle law and order and security questions, has come up with. It does not deal with the core of the problem but just suggests a security approach that has all the trappings of a witch hunt, where any person who is a Bengali speaker and a Muslim to boot has every chance of being a victim without access to the basics of justice proclaimed by those who so righteously defend India's human rights record. How many Guantanamo Bays does the Centre propose to set up?

Such an effort would create a nightmare for governments: law and order problems, media coverage of possible violation of rights (the media would go to town) and could snowball into a political crisis for any government. Minority groups would protest and even withdraw support to any government receiving their support. International human rights bodies and organizations would come down heavily against such exercises.

We also forget that the threat is from within and from our own deliberate neglect of the 'migrant-dominated regions'; visits there show islands and river bank areas with large populations without access to the basics of infrastructure: of course, no roads worth the name, no electricity, no schools or health clinics, no drinking water and no sanitation. If basics needs here are not met, we will have a radicalized population on our hands. Such a development would not depend on the number of madrasas which exist, as some pundits and politicians will have us believe. Madrasas are schools; their growth partly indicates the desperate effort of communities to give some education to their children in the absence of government schools and teachers.

My suggestion on migration has been in the public domain for some years – ID cards for all residents in the region based on the National Register of Citizens of 1951 and then Work Permits for all who have come after 1971. The Work Permits would not be an acceptance of permanent settlement nor would it confer the right to vote; it would confirm the temporary status of migrants and ensure they would not be eligible to the rights of a citizens—to acquire immovable property, move elsewhere in the country, marry locally and exercise a franchise.

The National Register of Citizens (NRC), 1951, remains the accurate basis of determining who lived where and since when, as well as matching census documents of 1971. But these suggestions may be too radical for any government to handle, even if led by the AGP or BJP. Ultimately, governments would choose the soft option and probably give citizenship or adult franchise rights to those who came until 1991.

Multipurpose, multicolor ID cards must be the basis for identifying who is an Indian and who is a resident alien and who is not. Work Permits should enable people to come in legally, stay for a year or two and go back. But without the ID cards, you cannot have a Work Permit scheme. This can be done through 'Smart' I-Cards which are developed using the latest software; a swipe of this card, much like a credit card, can confirm the person's identity and nationality.

At the moment, many illegals are de facto Indian citizens without even going through a minimal process which those born in India are required to; many of us are still without ID cards or the vote. I am not suggesting that these proposals will solve the problem but they represent a fresh approach to border management which is crucial in a region where 96 per cent of the borders are with other countries and 4 per cent with the rest of India. If we cannot solve the problems in the long-term, let us at least develop innovative and practical ways of managing them in the short and medium term.

As far as national security is concerned, there are elements in the migrants which are used by different groups—whether it is the insurgent groups in the North-east or outside of it, or their patrons from Pakistan or Bangladesh—but I do not see migrants per se as a security threat to India. In the immediate, they present a major economic and political pressure but not a security threat except for those elements that exist, either as 'sleepers' or as active agents seeking to destabilize the region in association with radicalized groups.

Often we gloss over the fact that some of the infiltrators

who pose a security threat are the very insurgent groups who proclaim their position against India and who keep slipping in and out of Bangladesh to step up their activities in the North-east.

In the long-term, the growing numbers of migrants and settlers have far-reaching social and political consequences. That is why we need political reservations for local communities in the State Assembly, based on the NRC and the 1971 census, which could be a permanent feature of the Constitution. Whatever the shape or size of the population, not less than 60 per cent should be reserved for the local communities. We may have a lot of problems in defining what local communities are, but there is enough work done through *The People of India* series, edited by Prof K.S. Singh, that could also form a basis for this.

Regional cooperation with Bangladesh leading to economic growth is important, because without building the nuts and bolts of infrastructure, we will continue to have this outflow. The best thing is to develop not just the border regions but a part of the hinterland as well so that roads, railways and waterways are used to transport goods and to develop infrastructure. Free Trade Zones and SEZs can be developed near the border to enable, among other industries, floriculture, meat, fruit and vegetable processing and to encourage and strengthen the economies on either side. Otherwise the spiral of poverty chasing poverty will be unstoppable.

This has been brought home to me in conversations with Bangladeshi farmers and fishermen who have travelled to Assam, worked in the state for twenty to thirty years, have voted in elections in Assam and have been patronized by

Assamese. They have worked across the state, as labourers and fishermen, farmers and contract labor.

Reflecting on the issues of inclusion and exclusion, Prof. Amartya Sen describes categorization is both a serious epistemic mistake and potentially a great ethical and political hazard, with far- reaching consequences for human rights. People do see themselves in many different ways. Thus, a Bangladeshi Muslim is not only a Muslim but also a Bengali and a Bangladeshi, not to mention the other identities that he/she may have, connected with class, gender, occupation, politics, food habits and so on. A Hindu from Nepal is not only a Hindu but also has ethnic and physical and political characteristics that have their own relevance along with other identities that make him/her what he/she is.

We need to look at the whole picture as well as the small fragments which comprise it, if we are to develop policies that not just make sense out of migration but help to manage it with sensitivity, competence, realism and understanding.

From the Inside, Looking East

'We are not islands, we cannot be. We cannot be exclusivist because we are part of a greater region,' the words of a former Prime Minister of India, Inder Kumar Gujral, resonated to a conference of the Association of South-East Asian nations. 'The food we eat, the clothes we wear, the languages we speak demonstrate that connectivity, of the past and one that continues.'

To take a few examples: the Mizos are part of the Kuki-Chins who reside also in Manipur and extensively in the Chin Hills and Sagaing Division of Myanmar. The Lisus are in Yunnan, Myanmar and Arunachal Pradesh. The Khasis talk of descent from Cambodia and speak Mon-Khmer. We have not less than 220 distinct ethnic groups in the North-east. The forests of teak and bamboo, depleted though they may be today and under acute stress, flow across international borders. One-time jungle trails and hill tracks are giving way to domestic and trans-national roads and highways which, though in different stages of construction and quality, often indifferent and poor, are bringing the markets and products of South-east Asia, and China especially, to our doorstep and into our homes. Engineers and planners are thinking of connecting Mizoram and the North-east by extension to the main port of Burma—Sittwe or Akiab in the Arakan, source of one of the richest oil and gas fields in Asia—via the Kaladyne River.

The strategy is simple, the aim is clear: with a network of road and water connections, India is seeking to bypass Bangladesh, which Delhi regards as being unhelpful to its economic and security interests, and have direct access to Myanmar's natural resources and enhance connectivity to South-east Asia. It would, in the process, give India not only a toehold of economic security in that region but help it establish a certain permanency of presence. For India's vision does not merely embrace access to South-east Asian markets but it also wants to send a clear and direct message to China that its influence in neighbouring Myanmar cannot go unchallenged.

This is a part of the 'Look East Policy (LEP), about which there is extensive and passionate argument among our political leaders and mandarins, more in New Delhi than in the North-east. In the region, it is the soft diplomacy that figures more prominently, with the promotion of a handful of cultural exchanges, seminars, tourism and investments. Economic muscle is crucial to this push, and Myanmar's association is seen by Delhi as critical to this effort.

To a great degree, this dependence on Myanmar and its generals, who have ruled since 1962, grows upon the fond hope that they will deliver to India the fuel to help meet its energy hunger and also tackle the insurgent groups based there which the might of the Indian State has not been able to neutralize. So the Government of India's so-called 'Look East Policy', launched in 1992 by the then Prime Minister P.V. Narasimha Rao, is not just about economic connectivity but also about gaining political advantage.

This is as much at the heart of India's unwillingness to directly come out against the military junta as anything else.

We have followed a policy that has moved from saying that developments in Myanmar are the internal concern of that country to joining other countries for the release of the pro-democracy leader Aung Sang Suu Kyi and for an open dialogue between the generals and the democrats. But even there we have hedged our bets.

This is why the Look East Policy which the External Affairs Minister Pranab Mukherjee described in June 2007 in Shillong as an approach to connect the North-east Region (NER) to South-east Asia lacks realism and vision. Indeed, his words were sharply contradicted by the Minister responsible for the North-east, the very articulate Mani Shankar Aiyar, who said that other parts of India had benefitted from the Look East Policy, not the North-east itself.

What is often overlooked in our understanding of such a policy is that it is not North-east specific. Delhi, in another assertion of paternalism, a precept that has coloured many of its approaches for the region, wants the LEP to work because it would also benefit the region. However, a senior official behind the most recent push says that is actually an 'Indian' foreign policy initiative that would benefit not just one region but many parts of India, which could take advantage of it. Although it is located partly in the region, it is not a pro-North-east policy. A brief look at the pathetically low figures for trade between the NER, Myanmar and South-east Asia will tell one side of the story. The other, more productive, side is visible from the trade statistics for this very region from Kolkata and Chennai.

Yet, whatever the implications of this approach, there cannot be a Look East Policy without a policy for Myanmar or Burma as it is still known in most of the world—for Burma straddles the well-travelled road to South-east Asia. It is there, a road block, a challenge, a situation of deep despair and acute poverty, and a brutal military that knows no other way or world and, as it showed in September 2007, is capable of turning viciously against men of the cloth, its own Buddhist monks and nuns. Conditions and developments in the country have a direct impact on the North-east, especially the border states of Mizoram, Manipur and Nagaland.

There is a growing level of military and economic collaboration between India and Myanmar and New Delhi keeps talking of how its reclusive neighbour is helping efforts to curb militancy by cracking down on North-eastern militant groups there. But not much is really happening on this front, barring the occasional desultory efforts against the Khaplang faction of the Nagas because to Myanmar these are not a real threat to security. In fact, there appears to be a comfortable relationship with some of them. Some years ago, senior leaders of a Manipuri insurgent group were briefly held by Burmese security forces at Tamu on the Indo-Burma border but quickly released, reportedly upon the payment of a huge sum of money and gems. Before their release, the BBC reported events in November 2001 in the following manner: 'The Inspector-General of the Indian Border Security Force (BSF) Manipur, Mr P.K. Mishra, told journalists that the Burmese have now informed them of the progress of the operations. Mr Mishra said (that) …

'more than 200 guerrillas of three separatist groups in Manipur, including seven of their leaders, have so far been arrested. They include the chairman of Manipur's largest separatist group, the United National Liberation Front (UNLF), Raj Kumar Meghen. The UNLF's General Secretary, Khaidem

Hamedou, its women wing chief, Nganbi Devi, and the chairman of a smaller Manipuri separatist group, the Kangleipak Communist Party, Th.Sanachou, have also been arrested. Mr Mishra said more than 1,600 weapons, including Chinese-made assault rifles, mortars, machine guns and rocket launchers, have been recovered from these six rebel camps. Large quantities of gold and gems worth millions of rupees and several printing machines producing fake Indian and foreign currencies have also been recovered, he said. Military officials say never before have so many weapons been seized during one single operation from any rebel group anywhere in the country. Burma and India agreed this year to coordinate military operations against separatist armies operating on the nearly 1,500 kilometres of border they share.'

That report went out on 11 November 2001. If this was the case, so loudly trumpetted at the time, then how did Raj Kumar Meghen (a scion of the Manipur royal family) and his colleagues get out of such a sticky situation? They continue to move about in Myanmar and parts of Manipur with relative ease. It is another reflection of the failure of India's blow hot-blow cold approach to Myanmar and its generals, hoping they will respond positively to its wooing, not realizing or unwilling to recognize that New Delhi has been outmaneuvered by Beijing with ease—India has neither China's economic muscle nor its political wile in Myanmarese matters.

Mizoram has felt the direct impact of the economic disaster and humanitarian crisis that is sweeping across Burma and its border regions. Some 80,000 Chins have migrated across the border in desperation, fleeing not just unstable political conditions but economic hardship. There has been a sharp change in Mizo attitudes towards the Chins—ranging from welcome and warmth in the mid-1990s to outright condemnation and hostility more recently. But we cannot move away from the reality that Mizoram has hosted a migrant population which is nearly one-tenth of its own size for this period of time.

Chins are good businessmen and businesswomen and hard working. The recent hostility towards them appears to be based on a feeling that they are responsible for an increase in crime rates in Mizoram, especially in theft and drugs. It is important to consider here that the reasons behind the outflow are militarization, lack of peace and under-development in Burma. If conditions at home were as attractive as conditions in India, people would not move. And that is one of the cardinal principles of out-migration, especially of refugees—people move away from unstable situations where they feel either at risk or under threat, from harsh political, environmental and economic situations.

A few years ago, I made a presentation to a Parliamentary Committee headed by Pranab Mukherjee on the problems of immigration and the objections to the Illegal Migrants (Determination by Tribunals) Act of 1983 (IMDT) in Assam. When I mentioned the in-migration of Chins in Mizoram, not one member of that panel was aware of the size of the problem or the gravity of the situation.

Many in the North-east are openly critical of corruption and poor governance. But often we fail to see the enormous benefits we have reaped over the years but which are clearly visible to our neighbours, who are denied access to basic infrastructure especially education and health facilities, as well as the core freedom to speak out and be heard by others and those in authority.

Democracy, however fractured and unrepresentative, is the key. Peace cannot progress into a participatory form of development without freedom of expression and freedom of choice, without a society that is not merely tolerant of dissent but respectful of it (and we have many dissenting voices in the North-east) and without local ownership of problems. Those at the village level, as noted elsewhere, need to be enabled to govern themselves through innovative processes instead of being controlled by those in district, state and national capitals.

My view is that India should not engage with the generals but engage with Myanmar and its people through a variety of forums; support the refugees, do not turn against them. For at some point in the future, they will be the leaders of a new Myanmar.

That is why the influx of Chins presents a great challenge to Mizo society but also highlights the potential and difficulties of democratic processes: we need to be understanding of those in distress. Targetting the Chins as criminals or branding them as harmful to society is not appropriate; action should be taken against criminal offenders but the conduct of a few should not be the reason for pressures on many.

A military junta in Myanmar does not work in our favour; it will work only to benefit its own interests, some of which will not coincide with ours. Thus, if they find something that works for them, even if it is against India's interests, they will move ahead on those lines.

We cannot prescribe democracy as a form of political rehabilitation for those societies or countries which we regard as 'difficult' but which we want to see reformed— Pakistan.

Afghanistan, Sri Lanka, Nepal and even Bhutan—and leave Myanmar out of that list. Does Delhi do so because Myanmar is so closely connected to the North-east? Because India needs its energy resources? Because it needs a policeman on its borders? These reasons are not good enough. Both in the short-term and the long-run, only a democratic and representative government in Myanmar will be helpful to India.

Peace and understanding, development and stability are the building blocks for progress and sustainable change. These flourish in transparent societies, not under the silence of shadow and fear. They are not limited to one area or state. That is another reason to support democracy in Burma, because it is of value and interest to us, it is in our self-interest. Not the whims of a few old generals who cannot see outside their limited world and want to destroy their people and country.

With the Look East Policy being bandied about so casually, there is much talk about cultural continuity, congruence and community with South-east Asia. But a real partnership does not emerge from cultural exchanges and exchanges of scholars: you need good hard research at its core. As a former Thai foreign minister said to me, 'What can help each other to grow, economically? We in South-east Asia do not know anything about the North-east—so how do you expect us to be connected to you? No investment will come in the presence of investor-unfriendly climate—with land laws and regulations where the entrepreneur cannot develop the way he wants to, for one, and where infrastructure is inadequate and security is difficult.'

To get information, to develop consistent and coherent

policies, we need good research. There is much talk about South-east Asia but not a single university in the entire region hosts a Centre for South-east Asian Studies. That one bare statistic belies the core of the Look East Policy—it lacks depth and true vision. If people are to learn about each other, they have to have a basis for that learning and understanding. Without learning the languages of our neighbours, distant and near, how will we connect? How will we communicate with future tourists and investors, if they come? Not everyone speaks English. These are simple steps that will help bridge the gap. There is no substitute for basic research and dissemination.

*

India has consistently thought that by engaging with the generals, supplying them weaponry and economic assistance, Yangon would play ball. And they would hack at the roots of the North-eastern insurgencies which are deeply entrenched on their side of the border. Delhi also thinks that if it is to get into the Big League and maintain, if not increase, its much vaunted growth rate of 9 per cent (while tens of millions subsist on one meal a day), then it needs access to the vast oil and gas reserves of Burma.

There are a few fallacies here. The first is that the Myanmar junta is prepared to help India by tackling the armed rebels there. This does not appear to be the case: groups from Manipur and even the United Liberation Front of Asom as well as Khaplang's group of the NSCN remain located on the borders with Myanmar. They move to conduct attacks and ambushes as well as extort and intimidate before going back.

This border is a tricky place; swamped with forests and swathed in hills, it is one of the most difficult terrains on earth to patrol and control. The Myanmar Army does not do much active military campaigning there. On the Indian side, however, to send another signal of Delhi's supportive intentions to the junta, there was a quiet clearing of the Chin National Army (CNA) camps at the Mizoram tri-junction of India, Myanmar and Bangladesh.

Of course, the CNA was also quietly tipped off about the operation and when the Mizoram police arrived, they found a deserted camp. The CNA is one of the Myanmarese insurgent groups which are semi-active in the Sagaigang Division of Burma on the other side of the border. But Myanmar exiles, migrants and refugee groups remain useful eyes and ears for Indian security agencies; many are located in the states along the border as well as in New Delhi. They are assets, not liabilities, for the days of the generals cannot continue without number.

On the economic front, India has much at stake with connectivity to the Bay of Bengal through the Kalodyne River which flows along Mizoram's border with Myanmar, as well as its active involvement in gas and oil exploration there. Again, this route has to be a multi-modal route, not merely river-based. Many also forget that China has far greater economic stakes and is well ahead of India in the energy hunt. It is setting up a 1,000 km Economic Development Corridor for gas, oil and highways between Yunnan Province and the Arakan of Burma.

This will protect its energy front by giving it direct access to Myanmar's oil and gas fields in the Bay of Bengal as well as to shipping routes. Indian naval bases in the Andamans and Nicbor archipelago will be under the Chinese scanner. In addition, there is a global dimension to their presence on the Myanmar coast—it will enable Beijing to challenge US control over the Straits of Molucca, one of the world's most imortant energy and trade routes. The port that the Chinese are building in Myanmar is a deep sea water port, unlike Sittwe, which the Indians are refurbishing. With that single stroke, the Chinese have defined who is ahead in the game for energy control, have gained security advantage and developed both political and economic power in Myanmar.

It is not that we should not negotiate for oil and gas, as Petroleum Minister Murli Deora or his predecessor Mani Shankar Aiyar have done. But Myanmar officials said that India took so long to take decisions that they virtually handed over the gas and oil deal on a platter to the Chinese.

Under a democratic, open regime in Myanmar, India's security and economic interests would be better protected and served. That is why we should continue to push the UN process, which even China and Russia, normally Myanmar's Big Boy friends who block every effort to castigate it at the Security Council, have accepted. In addition, once the internal process improves—despite the havoc of Cyclone Nargis and the junta's failure to get emergency relief to its people and blocking international efforts for weeks—India could consider initiating an effort to call an International Myanmar Conference, as has been done for other countries, bringing the conflicting sides and their neighbours to sit together at one table and hammer a way forward. It is not just pro-democracy or pro-regime; it is not whether we are on the side of Aung Sang Suu Kyi or not. It is whether we understand that while the military will continue to have a major role in

Myanmar in the future, whether regime changes take place, it must yield primacy to democratic forces. The army is too powerful to be ignored, like it or loathe it, and its interests would have to be 'protected'.

The generals of Myanmar live in a world of their own, filled with shadows of distrust and suspicion, and concern that the rest of the world wants to get them. It is also time we understood that for nearly fifty years, the people of that country have known only a military regime and none other; they too will be concerned and not a little suspicious of major changes. After all, Aung Sang's major colleagues in the National League for Democracy were once senior military generals who battled the ethnic armies in different provinces to a standstill.

Myanmar's turmoil is no longer its internal politics. It directly impacts our security and economic interests in the North-east, not to speak of larger national concerns, as well as its social fabric.

India needs to press forward with the opportunity provided by the UN dialogue process. If we are even a Regional Power (and an aspiring Big Power), then we have to behave like one, not back off when the crunch comes.

And, on a Personal Note, a Closing

A letter from a father

It's late and I watch you, my daughter, sleep the silence of an overwhelmed spirit, numbed by physical exhaustion, parties, friends, excitement, Santa Claus, gifts, fights, friendships, school.

The pressure of early morning school in the chill of a Delhi winter, when the snugness of a warm bed is luxury. Lousy, long, polluted Delhi mornings. A saving grace for me, anyway, is the jogs at the park opposite the IIT.

You can't hear me, child, but I need to tell you things you don't know about, not in any details, and I, supposed wordsmith and craftsman of phrase, find I don't have the words to reach out. The Right Words. I don't know why I am writing this. To calm my inner turmoil? Perhaps. To soothe your hurt aura? Perhaps. And those of others? Anyway, what are the Right Words?

I don't know. And where do I begin?

Last year, at this time, I was in Bhagalpur, contemplating the cruelty that people inflict on each other, Hindus and Muslims. The stench of graves, filled by rotting corpses of men, women and children. They were attacked in their homes, on village lanes and hacked in the bloodied village pond where they had sought refuge, thinking their attackers would not venture into the water.

Graves of groups of people, some with their hands tied behind their backs, are surfacing in Assam. Officials say they were buried alive. Others say that they were shot and then dumped in the graves for alleged crimes.

Nearly eight years ago, a few months before you were born, I walked on the killing fields of Nellie. And looked at the bodies of hundreds of men, women and children, many battered beyond recognition. Axed, speared, shot with muskets, pierced by arrows, knifed. The beginning of the shadow lines across the Brahmaputra Valley that are moving now towards a total eclipse of the tranquility, the good neighbourliness and the tolerance that has characterized Assamese society.

A few days ago, I was in Jehangirpur, in the southern outskirts of Delhi. How can one describe it but as a small village, with a single lane as its main road, shuttered by fear, violence and a curfew? I spent some time at the deserted, burned home of Ali Jan, a small shopkeeper.

A three-room home which hit the headlines because in one of those rooms, nine children suffocated. Suffocated is too easy a word. They died gasping for air, their lungs filled with smoke instead of oxygen. They coughed their lives out painfully, ultimately choking on their own vomit. It is not a pretty thought and some of them were younger than you, some were older, others were about your age. The police came and saved nine others, adults and children. Those who died were victims of an insane mob, bent on avenging an imaginary threat, a suspected insult.

Their shoes, caps and broken bangles were still there when I went that afternoon, mute witnesses to the horror. They are as wounding to my cynical spirit, weary of the hatred that have caused death and worse in every part of our subcontinent, as your tears. Our children are killed for no fault of their own, at Bhagalpur, at Jehangirpur, at Hyderabad. Spare the children, if no one else. What have they done except to be born as the sons and daughters of their fathers and mothers?

What kind of a world are we giving you? A hate-obsessed society? I look at the future and I am afraid, frightened by the demons that I see, the bitterness that has been unleashed and that you and your generation must battle and vanquish. For vanquish them you must, It is so unfair—you have to face and fight and pay for the collective folly of my generation in addition to the mistakes that yours will make. Each generation inherits the mistakes of the earlier one as well as its strengths. Ours individually are responsible for the lives we lead, the mess we make and the triumphs we secure. We cannot blame anyone else for our personal failures.

I'm meandering again. I think as I write. Or maybe I think to write. Is there a difference?

It's the end of the year, child, and time for your Christmas play. I watched you on stage at the school, singing and dancing with others. I missed that last year because I wasn't home. Your vibrancy came through, as did that of scores of others. But like all other fathers, I watched for my child. And afterwards you came, delighted to see me, running straight into my arms. Your hair flowing freely, your 'angel's' dress sweeping behind you, dodging your friends and other children on the school lawns. After a very long time.

I've been away a lot of times. On work. Too busy to attend to your small demands. Arriving too late to watch you on your cycle bursting with speed and energy. Be careful of the bends and blow that horn.

Maybe next year it'll be better. For all of us.

I guess I just have to be much more sensitive. Not that I'm not. But probably it's a selfish kind of sensitivity that looks more at how I'm affected by events, people, and pressures. I detest religious labels. I went to an Irish Brothers' Roman Catholic school in Shillong and grew up among pine trees, fresh air, friends of all groups and communities in a place where my father, a Socialist, worked as a tuberculosis specialist, loved for his compassion.

It's been a tough year for all of us. There's little enough of childhood in our country, where the heaviness of schoolbags of work to be done and checked, weigh so much on little spirits. And I haven't been much of a father, have I? Rarely been around when you needed me.

As I said, I don't know if any of this makes any sense to you. Or whether it will make sense in the future. Why am I saying all this? To exorcise inner demons? Perhaps. Demons that do not go away with all my jogging, my writing, my busyness.

Sleep well, my child, for you have many races to run, new worlds to conquer, hurdles to vault, pain and grief to overcome, joy and happiness to share. I've often been harsh with you, spoken and behaved abruptly. The memories shame me. I've not given you the time you need, the patient hearing you wanted, the unhurried love that is all you ask for. At times, I feel helpless, unsure of what to say or do.

I have no lessons to give, only experiences to share. And the sure knowledge that I am not what I thought I was.

If you can, my child, in the warmth of your love, the generosity of your questing spirit and the courage of your swift, fleeting feet–forgive me. And we shall face the world together.